ABOUT THE AUTHOR

An observer of the political scene from the vantage point of Washington, D. C., since 1933, M. B. Schnapper is the Political Science Editor of Public Affairs Press. He has contributed articles on national affairs to such publications as the New York Times, Washington Post, Christian Science Monitor, and Nation. Among the books he has prepared are The Truman Program, United Nations Agreements, and Public Housing in America. In the course of his varied career he has worked for the New York World, American Council on Education, and the President's Committee on Economic Security. From 1940 to 1950 he was Executive Secretary of the American Council on Public Affairs. In what he euphemistically calls his "spare time", Mr. Schnapper is now compiling a pictorial history of the Democratic Party and a volume entitled The Encyclopedia of Uncommon Knowledge.

GRAND OLD PARTY

GRAND OLD PARTY

THE FIRST HUNDRED YEARS
OF THE REPUBLICAN PARTY

A Pictorial History

M. B. SCHNAPPER

Public Affairs Press, Washington, D. C.

TO STEFAN LORANT
Pathbreaker

PREFACE

Although this book was prepared quite independently of the Republican Party and is in no sense an authorized work, it might well have been impossible to prepare without the generous cooperation of the Republican National Committee. The following members of the Committee's staff were especially considerate and helpful in this connection: Dr. Floyd McCaffree, Director of Research; Leroy H. Jones, Librarian; Robert Humphreys, Director of Public Relations; and Norris J. Nelson, assistant to Mr. Humphreys and Secretary of the Republican Centennial Committee.

In the planning stage, Postmaster General Arthur Summerfield, former Chairman of the Republican National Committee, and his aide, Joseph Cooper, made a number of valuable suggestions, but their interest was quite informal and unofficial.

At the Library of Congress, Milton Kaplan, co-author of "Presidents on Parade", went far beyond the line of bureaucratic duty in tracking down fugitive material, in offering expert counsel, and in rescuing the author from strangulation by the tens of thousands of fascinating illustrations in the Prints and Photos Division. His colleagues, Hirst Milhollen and Miss Virginia Daiker, also extended unfailing courtesies. Despite the author's frequent and perhaps unreasonable requests, the Library's Photo Duplication Service was patient, kind, and efficient—thanks to the smooth running supervision of Donald Holmes.

Others in Washington who were helpful in locating valuable materials were Miss Josephine Cobb of the National Archives; James Macgill, Assistant Director of the National Gallery of Art; Miss Lillian Cash of the National Park Service; H. L. Raul, Director of the Department of Interior Museum; and Miss Norma Hazeltine of the Bureau of Land Management.

In New York the Frick Art Reference Gallery and the New York Historical Society were exceedingly cooperative.

Among those who gave generously of their advice in editorial matters were Eugene Berlin, Reed Harris, E. C. Teodorescu, Karl E. Gilmont, Allen Harpine, and Arthur G. Powell.

To the persons and agencies listed below the author is deeply indebted for special assistance on the subjects specified:

Origin of the Republican Party: Wisconsin Historical Society, Madison, Wisconsin; Robert C. Born, Mayor of Ripon, Wisconsin; Jackson Public Library of Jackson, Michigan. Abraham Lincoln: Lincoln Museum, Washington, D. C. Andrew Johnson: Andrew Johnson National Monument, Greenville, Tennessee. Ulysses S. Grant: Major General Ulysses S. Grant 3rd, Alexandria, Virginia; Grant Museum, Point Pleasant, Ohio. Rutherford B. Hayes: Watt Marchman, Director of the Hayes Memorial Library, Fremont, Ohio. James A. Garfield:

Ohio State Archaeological and Historical Society, Columbus, Ohio. Chester A. Arthur: Vermont Historical Society, Montpelier, Vermont; Nebraska Historical Society, Lincoln Nebraska. William McKinley: National William McKinley Memorial Museum, Niles, Ohio. Theodore Roosevelt: Theodore Roosevelt Association, New York City; American Museum of Natural History, New York City. William Howard Taft: Elizabeth Kern, former secretary of Senator Robert A. Taft; Taft Collection in the Library of Congress. Charles Evans Hughes: Mrs. Chauncey Waddell and Mrs. William T. Gossett, daughters of the late Chief Justice. Warren G. Harding: President Harding Museum, Marion, Ohio. Calvin Coolidge: Vermont Historical Society, Montpelier, Vermont. Herbert Hoover: State Historical Society of Iowa, Iowa City, Iowa; Herbert Hoover Birthplace Society, West Branch, Iowa. Alfred M. Landon: Kansas State Historical Society, Topeka, Kansas. Wendell Willkie: Mrs. Wendell Willkie; Elwood Public Library, Elwood, Indiana. Thomas E. Dewey: Harry J. O'Donnell, Executive Assistant to Governor Dewey, Albany, New York. Dwight D. Eisenhower: William Adam, U.S. Department of Defense; Eisenhower Foundation, Abilene, Kansas; Citizens Committee for Eisenhower, Washington, D. C.

Of the hundreds of books consulted, the following were well nigh indispensable and deserve far more than mere bibliographical mention: "Presidents on Parade", Milton Kaplan and Hirst Milhollen, Macmillan, 1948; "The American Past", Roger Butterfield, Simon and Schuster, 1947; "The Presidency", Stefan Lorant, Macmillan, 1951; "The Republican Party: A History", William Starr Myers, Century, 1928; "The Republican Party, 1854-1904", Francis Curtis, Putnam's, 1904.

Some fine art touches and retouches were provided by Mrs. Blanche Theeman and Ivan Stear.

Last, but certainly not least, is my indebtedness to Blanche, Eric, and Amy. They truly sacrificed much for the sake of the Republican Party.

M. B. SCHNAPPER

CONTENTS

CHAPTER ONE   9

CHAPTER TWO   21

CHAPTER THREE   31

CHAPTER FOUR   81

CHAPTER FIVE   105

CHAPTER SIX   143

CHAPTER SEVEN   169

CHAPTER EIGHT   189

CHAPTER NINE   205

CHAPTER TEN   219

CHAPTER ELEVEN   243

CHAPTER TWELVE   283

CHAPTER THIRTEEN   323

CHAPTER FOURTEEN   347

CHAPTER FIFTEEN   361

CHAPTER SIXTEEN   387

CHAPTER SEVENTEEN   411

CHAPTER EIGHTEEN   439

CHAPTER NINETEEN   453

CHAPTER TWENTY   467

CHAPTER TWENTY-ONE   481

CREDITS   511

INDEX   517

The Ripon, Wisconsin, schoolhouse in which the Republican Party was born on March 20, 1854. "We went in . . . Whigs, Free Soilers, and Democrats," recalled Alvan E. Bovay. "We came out of it Republicans." Widespread dissatisfaction with existing parties developed when the passage of the Kansas-Nebraska Bill permitted the extension of slavery into the Kansas and Nebraska territories. The major immediate objective of the founders of the new party was to prevent the spread of slavery.

The United States of America in 1854. The lightly shaded areas were slave states; dark areas were free states. Indicated in the center are the outlines of Kansas and Nebraska.

9

Plans for the creation of the Republican Party were originally drawn up at meetings held in Ripon's First Congregational Church on February 28 and, evidently, on March 1, 1854.

Prime mover in the formation of the Republican Party was Major Alvan E. Bovay, a prominent Ripon Whig. During a visit to New York City in 1852, he broached the need for the party in a talk with editor Horace Greeley. Whether he or, as some contend, Greeley first used the term Republican is unclear, but there can be no doubt that Bovay deserves full credit for organizing the meetings held in Ripon. In a letter sent to Greeley two days before the February 28th meeting, Bovay tersely explained why he liked the term Republican: "It is the only one that will serve all purposes present and future—the only one that will live and last." A lawyer by occupation, Bovay held the rank of Major during the Civil War.

The first Republican meeting at which a formal platform was adopted was the historic "under the oaks" convention held in Jackson, Michigan, on July 6, 1854. So many persons attended that adjournment to a near-by grove became necessary when the town's largest hall proved too small. It was resolved "that . . . in view of the necessity of battling for the first principles of Republican government, and against the schemes of an aristocracy, the most revolting and oppressive with which the earth was ever cursed, or man debased, we will cooperate and be known as Republicans until the contest be terminated." A full state ticket was nominated.

LIBERTY, THE FAIR MAID OF KANSAS—IN THE HANDS OF THE "BORDER RUFFIANS".

High-handed treatment of Kansas is here blamed upon the leaders of the Democratic Party. Robbing a "free-soiler" at the left are James Buchanan and trouser-patched Secretary of State William Marcy. In the center the "fair maid" of Kansas pleads with President Franklin Pierce while Senator Lewis Cass looks on lasciviously. The scalper at right is Senator Stephen A. Douglas.

12

Pro-slavery sympathizers from Missouri—"Border Ruffians"—flocked into Kansas shortly after enactment of the controversial Kansas-Nebraska Bill repealed the Missouri Compromise.

Violence broke out as the "Border Ruffians" encountered abolitionists. Enraged by the pillaging of Lawrence, John Brown and his sons sought revenge through warfare against slaveholders.

Free State supporters in Kansas drew up a constitution of their own at a Topeka meeting (above) in December 1855, two months after pro-slavery elements organized a territorial government with the support of "Border Ruffians" and "squatters" from Missouri and other nearby states.

Federal troops were ordered out by President Franklin Pierce to break up meetings and protest of Free Staters following recognition of the pro-slavery government in the Kansas Territory

The forces behind the young Republican Party won a major victory on February 2, 1856, when Nathaniel Banks, a Massachusetts Free Soiler who had vigorously opposed the Kansas-Nebraska Bill, was elected Speaker of the House of Representatives over William Aiken, a South Carolina slaveholder, after an unprecedented stalemate in national affairs. For two months the lower chamber had been deadlocked while 133 ballot contests for the Speakership were conducted.

The first national meeting of the new party was held in Pittsburgh's Lafayette Hall in February 1856. A call was issued for a Presidential convention in Philadelphia in June of the same year.

In May 1856, several days after delivering his blistering speech "The Crime Against Kansas", Senator Charles Sumner of Massachusetts was beaten insensible on the floor of the upper chamber by Rep. Preston S. Brooks. The attack was made by Brooks for personal as well as Carolina had been strongly castigated in Sumner's speech. Originally a Free Soil Democrat, Sumner became an outstanding member of the Republican Party. "Next to Lincoln, he undoubtedly did more to win freedom for the colored race than any other man," according to histo-

Violence again broke out in Congress—this time in the House of Representatives in 1858—during arguments over slavery and Kansas. It started when Rep. Keitt of South Carolina called Rep. Grow of Pennsylvania "a black Republican puppy"; a general brawl followed.

B. GRATZ BROWN.

HON. GEO. S. BOUTWELL

HENRY WILSON

HON. ELIHU B. WASHBURN

They were leading **figures of** the Republican Party in the 1850's and 1860's.

HON. RICHARD J. OGLESBY

HON. CHARLES SUMNER

HON. LYMAN TRUMBULL

HON. HAMILTON FISH

Hamilton Fish and Charles Sumner were prominent in the fight against slavery.

As the elections of 1856 approached, the issues of the day became sharper and the youthful Republican Party gained strength.

Dashing, audacious John Charles Fremont, the first Presidential candidate of the Republican Party, undoubtedly would have been elected had he been willing to run on the Democratic ticket in 1856. Tendered the nomination by the leaders of both organizations, he decided to align himself with the new party even though Democratic backing would have practically guaranteed his occupancy of the White House.

One of the most colorful personalities in American history, Fremont captured the popular imagination with his daring-do as explorer and Army officer. During his late twenties and early thirties, he headed trail-blazing expeditions which opened up the west. In 1846 he helped California obtain independence from Mexico and was appointed the first governor of the territory. Involvement in a quarrel with General Stephen Kearny later led to his removal and court martial, but sentence was remitted by President Polk. Subsequently Fremont made a fortune via gold discoveries in California. In 1849 the new state elected him one of its two first U.S. Senators. Although his opposition to slavery cost him his reelection, it greatly enhanced his reputation as a national figure and contributed to his nomination by the newly formed Republican Party.

A photograph of Fremont (extreme right) with his wife and two friends in 1861. When the Civil War broke out Fremont was made a Major General and given command of Union forces in the west. However, his premature emancipation of slaves and confiscation of rebel property led to less important assignments during the conflict.

Like her husband, Mrs. Jessie Benton Fremont was a person of unusual talents. She prepared most of the reports of her husband's explorations.

23

In the "Bear Flag Revolt" of Californians against Mexico's government in 1846, Fremont figured conspicuously.

Climaxing his exploration of the Rocky Mountains, Fremont raised the American flag on one of the highest peaks.

With a small band of men, Fremont undertook daring explorations of the western territories.

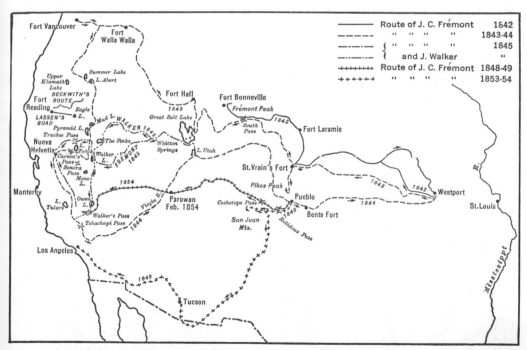

Fremont brought back the first detailed information about the geography, geology, and meteorology of the west. His reports, written with his wife's help, greatly facilitated settlement.

Responding with "the hot-eyed fervor of a revival meeting", delegates to the first Republican convention, held in Philadelphia in June 1856, "went mad with joy, shouting, and cheering" when Fremont was nominated on the second ballot. Selection of Senator William L. Dayton of New Jersey as his running mate almost went unnoticed. The campaign that followed took on many of the characteristics of a holy crusade. Among those who sang praises of Fremont and the new party were such literary lights as Ralph Waldo Emerson, John Greenleaf Whittier, Walt Whitman, Washington Irving, Henry Ward Beecher, and Horace Greeley. The initial platform of the party opposed extension of slavery, advocated the admission of Kansas as a free state, and endorsed homestead legislation.

"Let us, in building our new party, plant ourselves on the rock of the Declaration of Independence and the gates of hell shall not prevail against us," declared Abe Lincoln in 1856.

Only 43, Fremont was one of the youngest Presidential candidates in American history. Campaign posters made much of this and did not neglect the attractiveness of his young wife. By contrast, the Democratic Presidential nominee, James Buchanan, was associated with "Old Fogeyism".

JOHN C. FREMONT. THE REPUBLICANS CHOICE FOR PRESIDENT **AND** **Wᴹ. L. DAYTON.** VICE PRESIDENT FROM 1857 TO 1861.

Their ticket aroused fervent support. "Newspapers of the north, midwest, northwest, and west published Fremont's praises in endless eulogistic articles," relates Irving Stone. "Poetry was written, songs composed, his portrait hung in shopwindow and home, campaign biographies were widely read, torchlight parades and mass meetings were held in all non-slave cities. Women, for the first time, campaigned, sang songs . . . young men's clubs called 'The Wide Awakes' spread across the land; roads were clogged with every manner of vehicle carrying enthusiasts to town to work for Free Soil, Free Men, Fremont and Victory."

GREAT EXCITEMENT!!

Arrival in this City of

THE NONDESCRIPT!

OR

WOOLLY HORSE

And will be exhibited

ONCE IN A WHILE,

At the Hut, corner of Asylum and High Streets, until Nov. 4th, previous to taking its departure for Salt River.

Nature seems to have exhausted all her ingenuity in the production of this

WONDERFUL AND ASTONISING ANIMAL,

He is a complex, made up of the Elephant, Deer, Horse, Jackass, Buffalo, Camel, Calf, and Negro! Is the full size of the Horse. Has a negro head, abolition body, tail of the snake, and feet like an elephant. A fine black curled WOOL covers his head and EYES, and he easily bounds to the highest kind of political majorities at a single jump. Naturalists and Political Antiquarians say that his antecedents are but LITTLE KNOWN in Natural History. Philosophers Beecher, Bennett, and others have labored hard to give some scientific diagnosis of this truly

WONDERFUL ANIMAL,

But no two of them agree as to his origin, religion, character and habits. He is indisputably, and undoubtedly,

Nature's First and Last of his Species.

He will be exhibited only in the evening, as that is the only time when he exhibits his wonderful strength of lungs and limbs. He assumes during the day a comatose and sleepy state, apparently recruiting his energies for his extra-

---

FOR

SALT RIVER!

DIRECT.!!

THE FAST SAILING STEAMER

BLACK REPUBLICAN!

Capt. J. C. FREMONT, "No. 1,"

Has her Freight on board, and will have quick dispatch on

NOVEMBER 4TH, 1856.

The following is a list of the Officers and Crew for the voyage:

ENGINEERS.	MATE.
"FREE LOVE" GREELY,	"DU DAH" DAY
"FOXY" RAYMOND.	STEWARDS.
FIREMEN.	"SAUNEY" BENNETT.
"HOLY RIFLE" BEECHER,	"LET THE UNION SLIDE" BANKS.
FRED DOUGLASS.	
PURSERS.	CHAMBERMAID.
KANSAS WAR COMMITTEE.	MRS. "BLEEDING KANSAS."

A great number of "Political Parsons," who have stolen the Livery of Heaven to serve the Devil in, will be on board.

A patent "Caliope" is engaged, and will give several "Shrieks for Kansas."

The "Shaking Quakers" from Pennsylvania, "who did not vote" on the 14th inst., will amuse the Company during the trip.

This Boat is of light draft, and will reach nearer the "Head Waters of SALT RIVER" than any other craft.

☞ NO NIGGERS ALLOWED ON BOARD. ☜

For Passage only, apply to the President of the Fremont Club, at the "HUT."

N. B.—Passengers are to be on board at 5 o'clock. After that hour they will be brought on board on Litters, Wheelbarrows and Coffins.

P. S.—Ship Stores must be sent on board as early as possible, for a 4 years' cruise.

Like other candidates for public office, before and since, Fremont was subjected to vilification by opposition propaganda. The "Woolly Horse" referred to at left above was a dig at the Republican Party. Supporters depicted in cartoon below include a Communist and a free love advocate.

28

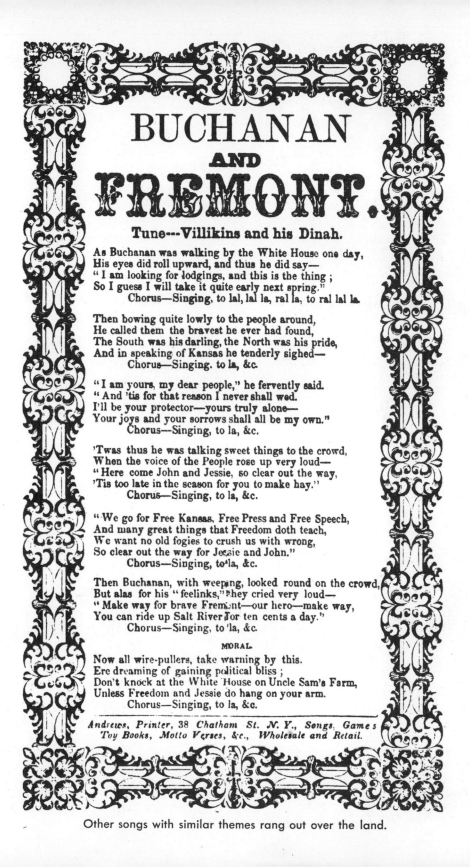

BUCHANAN
AND
FREMONT.

Tune---Villikins and his Dinah.

As Buchanan was walking by the White House one day,
His eyes did roll upward, and thus he did say—
"I am looking for lodgings, and this is the thing ;
So I guess I will take it quite early next spring."
    Chorus—Singing, to lal, lal la, ral la, to ral lal la.

Then bowing quite lowly to the people around,
He called them the bravest he ever had found,
The South was his darling, the North was his pride,
And in speaking of Kansas he tenderly sighed—
    Chorus—Singing. to la, &c.

"I am yours, my dear people," he fervently said.
"And 'tis for that reason I never shall wed.
I'll be your protector—yours truly alone—
Your joys and your sorrows shall all be my own."
    Chorus—Singing, to la, &c.

'Twas thus he was talking sweet things to the crowd,
When the voice of the People rose up very loud—
"Here come John and Jessie, so clear out the way,
'Tis too late in the season for you to make hay."
    Chorus—Singing, to la, &c.

"We go for Free Kansas, Free Press and Free Speech,
And many great things that Freedom doth teach,
We want no old fogies to crush us with wrong,
So clear out the way for Jessie and John."
    Chorus—Singing, to la, &c.

Then Buchanan, with weeping, looked round on the crowd,
But alas for his "feelinks," they cried very loud—
"Make way for brave Fremont—our hero—make way,
You can ride up Salt River for ten cents a day."
    Chorus—Singing, to 'la, &c.

MORAL

Now all wire-pullers, take warning by this.
Ere dreaming of gaining political bliss ;
Don't knock at the White House on Uncle Sam's Farm,
Unless Freedom and Jessie do hang on your arm.
    Chorus—Singing, to la, &c.

*Andrews, Printer, 38 Chatham St. N. Y., Songs, Games
Toy Books, Motto Verses, &c., Wholesale and Retail.*

Other songs with similar themes rang out over the land.

Taciturn Senator William L. Dayton secured the Vice Presidential
nomination over an eloquent Illinoisan named Abraham Lincoln.

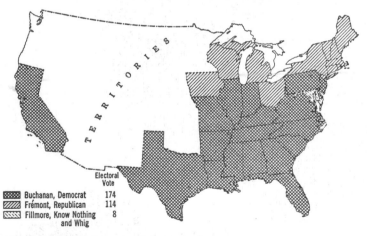

Electoral
Vote

Buchanan, Democrat   174
Frémont, Republican   114
Fillmore, Know Nothing   8
        and Whig

Considering that the Republican Party was only two years old
at the time, that it had ineffective organization in many states,
and that it could hardly expect any support from the South,
Fremont did extremely well.   He received 114 electoral votes to
174 for James Buchanan, the successful Democratic candidate.
By 1858, significantly, a plurality of the members of the House
of Representatives were Republicans and several states (including
Maine and Wisconsin) had elected Republican Governors.

The nation's first Republican President, Abraham Lincoln became closely identified with the newly formed party in 1856, receiving 110 votes for the Vice Presidential nomination at the convention which selected Fremont and Dayton. "Two years ago," Lincoln recalled in 1858, "the Republicans of the nation mustered over thirteen hundred thousand strong. We did this under the single impulse of resistance to a common danger, with every external circumstance against us. Of strange, discordant, and even hostile elements, we gathered from the four winds, and formed and fought the battle through, under the constant hot fire of a disciplined, proud, and pampered enemy."

Lincoln's humble log cabin birthplace near Hodgenville, Kentucky.

Abe was twenty when he helped his father build this home in Illinois.

A painting of Lincoln with his family in 1862: Tad, the President, Robert, and Mrs. Lincoln

The youngster depicted in the portrait hanging near Robert is Willie, who had died of a "bilious fever" earlier in the year. A fourth son, Edward, passed away in 1846, the same year Willie was born. Tad died at eighteen. Robert lived to the ripe old age of eighty-three; he served as Secretary of War during the Garfield and Arthur administrations.

Mrs. Lincoln, the former Mary Todd, was the daughter of a well-to-do Kentucky merchant. She is seen at the left in a photograph taken by Mathew Brady.

I was born Feb. 12. 1809, in Hardin county, Kentucky.
My parents were both born in Virginia, of undistin-
guished families — second families, perhaps I should say.
My mother, who died in my
tenth year, was of a family of the name of Hanks,
some of whom now reside in Adams, and others
in Macon counties, Illinois — My paternal grandfather, Abraham Lincoln, emigrated from Rock-
ingham county, Virginia, to Kentucky, about 1781 or
2, where, a year or two later, he was killed by
indians, not in battle, but by stealth, when he
was laboring to open a farm in the forest —
His ancestors, who were quakers, went to Virginia
from Berks county, Pennsylvania — An effort to
identify them with the New-England family of the same name
ended in nothing more definite, than a similarity
of Christian names in both families, such as
Enoch, Levi, Mordecai, Solomon, Abraham, and
the like —

My father, at the death of his father, was
but six years of age; and he grew up,
litterally without education. He removed
from Kentucky to what is now Spencer county, Indiana, in my eighth year — We reached our new home
about the time the State came into the Union — It
was a wild region, with many bears and other
wild animals, still in the woods — There I grew
up. There were some schools, so called; but no
qualification was ever required of a teacher, beyond
"readin, writin, and cipherin"
reading, writing, and arithmetic to the Rule of
Three — If a straggler supposed to understand latin,
happened to sojourn in

The story of Lincoln's life in his own words and handwriting.

the neighborhood, he was looked upon as a wizzard— There was absolutely nothing to excite ambition for education. Of course when I came of age I did not know much— Still somehow, I could read, write, and cipher to the Rule of Three; but that was all— I have not been to school since— The little advance I now have upon this store of education, I have picked up from time to time under the pressure of necessity—

I was raised to farm work, which I continued till I was twenty-two— At twenty-one I came to Illinois, and passed the first year in Illinois— Macon County— Then I got to New Salem (then, at that time in Sangamon, now in Menard County, where I remained a year as a sort of Clerk in a store— Then came the Black-Hawk war; and I was elected a Captain of Volunteers— a success which gave me more pleasure than any I have had since— I went the campaign, was elated, ran for the Legislature the same year (1832), and was beaten— the only time I ever have been beaten by the people— The next, and three succeeding biennial elections, I was elected to the Legislature— I was not a candidate afterwards. During this Legislative period I had studied law, and removed to Springfield to practice it— In 1846 I was once elected to the lower House of Congress— Was not a candidate for re-election— From 1849 to 1854, both

This autobiographical sketch was written in December 1859.

inclusive, practiced law more assiduously than ever before—Always a whig in politics, and generally on the whig electoral tickets, making active canvasses. I was losing interest in politics, when the repeal of the Missouri Compromise aroused me again. What I have done since then is pretty well known.

If any personal description of me is thought desirable, it may be said, I am, in height, six feet, four inches, nearly; lean in flesh, weighing, on an average, one hundred and eighty pounds; dark complexion, with coarse black hair, and grey eyes—no other marks or brands recollected—

Hon. J. W. Fell.   Yours very truly
                                    A. Lincoln

                    Washington. D.C. March 20. 1872
We the undersigned hereby certify, That the foregoing statement is in the hand writing of Abraham Lincoln.
                    David Davis
                    Lyman Trumbull
                    Charles Sumner

The original was sent to the Illinois Republican State Committee.

The fence rails Lincoln split in his youth became popular symbols when he ran for the Senate seat. In a vivid firsthand account of Lincoln the politician, Horace White, Secretary of the Republican State Committee of Illinois while Abe was active in campaign work, relates: "He was one of the shrewdest politicians of the state. Nobody had more experience in that way; nobody knew better than he what was passing in the minds of the people. Nobody knew better how to turn things to advantage politically, and nobody was readier to take such advantage, provided it did not involve dishonorable means. He could not cheat people out of their votes any more than out of their money. The Abraham Lincoln that some people have pictured to themselves, sitting in his dingy law office, working over his cases till the voice of duty roused him, never existed. If this had been his type, he never would have been called at all."

In the stirring debates of 1858 between Lincoln and Democrat Stephen A. Douglas a seat in the U.S. Senate was at stake. Abe lost the Senatorship, but won the Presidency. In addressing the convention which nominated him for the Senate, he spoke prophetically: "A house divided against itself cannot stand; I believe this government cannot endure permanently half slave and half free."

hey were considered the most eligible candidates for the Republican Party nomination in 1860. Senator **William H.** Seward of New York (top center), then the indisputable leader of the party, seemed to have the best prospects; he later served as Secretary of State under Lincoln and Johnson. Portrayed in the left panel are Edward Bates, a Missouri jurist who became Lincoln's Attorney General; William Pennington, Speaker of the House of Representatives; Salmon P. Chase, former Governor of Ohio, who became Secretary of the Treasury; and John C. Fremont, the party's Presidential nominee in 1856. At the right are Nathaniel P. Banks, Governor of Massachusetts; John McLean, Associate Justice of the Supreme Court; Simon Cameron, "favorite son" of Pennsylvania, who was appointed Lincoln's first Secretary of War; John Bell, who became the candidate of the Constitutional Union Party; and Cassius M. Clay, a Kentucky abolitionist who later served as Minister to Russia.

tocky Senator Hannibal Hamlin of Maine was picked s Lincoln's running mate. Geographical considerations and his anti-slavery record made him an excellent choice for the Vice Presidency. He was elected Governor of Maine on the Republican ticket in 1857.

When Lincoln's name was placed before the Chicago convention of 1860, according to a contemporary report, "the response was absolutely terrific . . . the uproar was beyond description.
Imagine all the hogs ever slaughtered in Cincinnati giving their death squeals together, a score
of big steam whistles going, and you conceive something of the same nature". And when, on
the third ballot, it became clear that Lincoln would win the nomination, "There was a moment's
silence. The nerves of thousands, which through the hours of deep suspense had been subjected
to terrible tension, relaxed, and as deep breaths of relief were taken, there was a noise in the
Wigwam like the rush of a great wind in the van of a storm—and in another breath, the storm
was there. There were thousands cheering with the energy of insanity."

An exterior view of the specially built "Wigwam" in which Lincoln was nominated for President.

Their platform was substantially similar to that drawn up by the Republican Party in 1856. New planks advocated homestead grants for western settlers and a protective tariff.

Standing in the doorway of his Springfield home, Lincoln greeted supporters in August 1860, while his wife looked on. "Republicans are for both the man and the dollar," Abe declared during the campaign, "but in case of conflict the man before the dollar."

Grand procession of Republican "Wide Awakes" in New York. Wearing glazed caps and o

cloth capes as protection against drippings from their torches, they staged colorful parades.

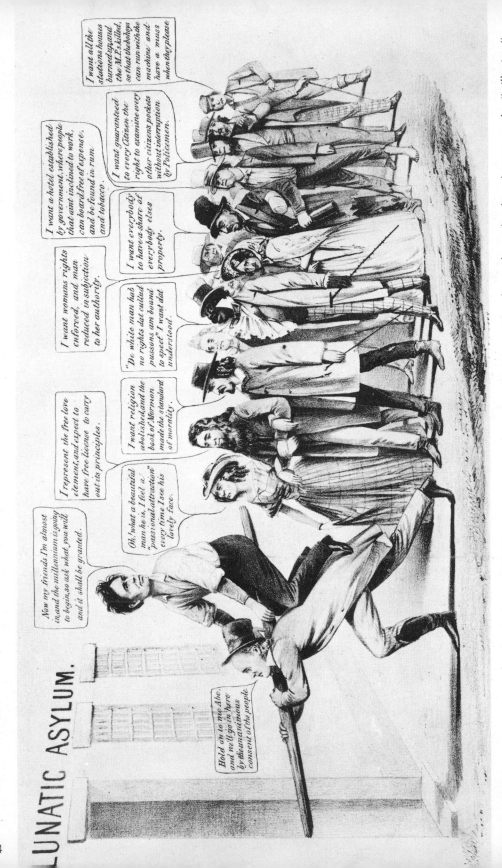

44

"The Republican Party Going to the Right House" (above) was probably the most defamatory cartoon about Lincoln in the 1860 campaign. Journalist Horace Greeley is shown leading the way to the "millenium" for advocates of free love, atheism, and even women's rights.

This lithograph shows rivals Bell, Douglas, and Breckinridge getting some advice on how to hit a Presidential home run.

In "**The Political Gymnasium**" above, Edward Everett, Vice Presidential candidate of the Constitutional Union Party, is "upholding" his running mate, John Bell, while Lincoln-supporter Horace Greeley struggles to get astride the nomination for Governor of New York. In the foreground, editor James W. Webb is shown turning somersaults. The boxers are Douglas and Breckinridge, competing Democratic candidates. At the right is Senator Seward, not yet recovered from the injuries he suffered in falling from the Republican nomination bar.

"**Letting the Cat Out of the Bag**" portrays Senator Charles Sumner as the cause of party discord. His abolitionist views on slavery tended to alienate the moderate elements supporting Lincoln.

The artist was **confident** Abe could easily swallow his Democratic opponents—"Soft Shell" Stephen A. Douglas and "Hard Shell" John C. Breckinridge.

Lincoln vs. Douglas in a cartoon entitled "The Undecided Political Prize Fight".

Although greatly disappointed because he failed to receive the nomination, Senator William H. Seward became one of Lincoln's strongest supporters. The caricature at the left shows him in a Shakespearean adaptation of the costume worn by the "Wide Awakes" in their parades.

In a vivid, if prejudiced, description of Senator Douglas, journalist Murat Halstead wrote: "And here, coming from the cloak-room on the Democratic side, is a queer little man, canine head and duck legs—everybody knows the Little Giant—he looks conscious of being looked at—as he makes pretentious strides of about eighteen inches each, toward his chair . . . The Little Giant wears his black hair long, but it is getting thin, and is not the great tangled mass we saw on his neck a few years ago."

A Vanity Fair cartoonist pictured Democratic candidate Douglas as "Aminadab Sleek", a ludicrous character in a popular comedy of the period.

"It [the Republican Party] is a party of one idea," Seward declared in a speech he gave in Rochester, "but that is a noble one — an idea that fills and expands all generous souls; the idea of equality—the equality of all men before human tribunals and human laws, as they are all equal before the divine tribunal and divine laws."

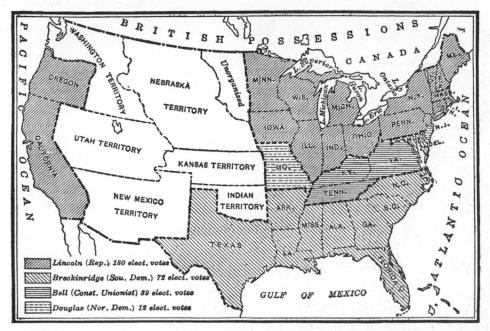

Lincoln's victory over his rivals gave him a wide majority in the 1860 electoral vote. However, news of his election was interpreted as a signal for secession.

In this cartoon, Democratic candidates Breckinridge and Douglas are being informed by Uncle Sam that he has decided to choose Abe Lincoln for the White House job.

The admission of Kansas into the Union as a Free State on January 29, 1861, was heralded by President-elect Lincoln at Philadelphia's Independence Hall on Washington's Birthday. In commemoration of the event, he hoisted a flag with 34 stars.

Below is Ben Day's interpretation of the "Crittenden Compromise" as an attempt to force an obnoxious measure upon the Republican Party. Narrowly defeated in the Senate by a vote of 20 to 19 two days before Lincoln's inauguration, the bill would have put federal sanction upon slavery in the south.

Two views of the inaugural procession on its way to the Capitol. Flanked by armed, high-hatted cavalrymen, President-elect Lincoln rode with President James Buchanan in an open carriage. Sharpshooters were stationed in many of the windows along Pennsylvania Avenue.

Aging Chief Justice Roger B. Taney administered the oath of office to Lincoln at a tense moment in the nation's history. Greatly disturbed by the secession movement of 1860-61, Lincoln's major concern was preservation of the Union without bloodshed. "We are not enemies, but friends," he assured the South in his inaugural address. On a nearby platform were four future Presidents: Rutherford B. Hayes, James A. Garfield, Chester A. Arthur, and Benjamin Harrison.

Sharpshooters were stationed around the still unfinished Capitol as Lincoln delivered his eloquent inaugural address.

In describing a reception Lincoln held in the Capitol shortly before his inauguration, Albert G. Riddle wrote: "He was in wonderful spirits, surrounded by twenty or thirty admiring adherents, standing at his full height, which from his lack of breadth, always seemed exaggerated. His face was fairly radiant, his wit and humor at flood-tide. His marvelous faculty of improvising illustrated stories was at its best."

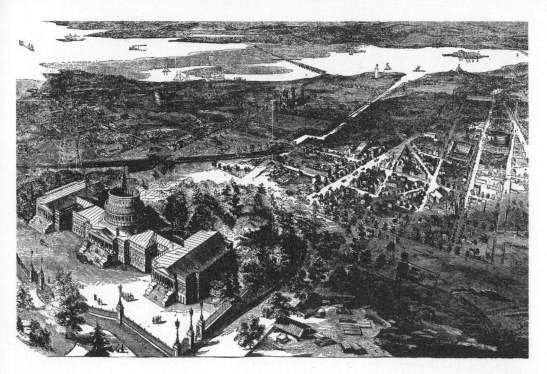

Washington, D. C., was still a city of "magnificent distances" with muddy and poorly lighted streets.   Above is a sketch drawn in 1861; note the old canal and the unfinished Capitol. Below is a print of the White House when Lincoln moved into it; sightseers moved about freely.

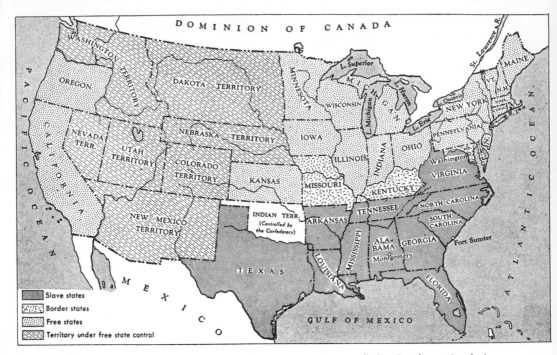

By the late spring of 1861 the **darkened** states constituted the Southern Confederacy.

Troops quartered in the Capitol prepared to defend Washington, D. C., from attack.

Upon finding some of his errant pupils at the **secession** swimming hole, Schoolmaster **Lincoln** offers to forgive and forget, but unruly **South Carolina** persists in behaving disagreeably.

Dr. Lincoln's homeopathic treatment: "Now, Miss Columbia, if you will follow my prescriptions, which are of an extremely mild character, but which your old nurse, Mrs. Buchanan, seems to have been so averse to, I have no doubt but that the Union will be restored to position, health, and vigor."

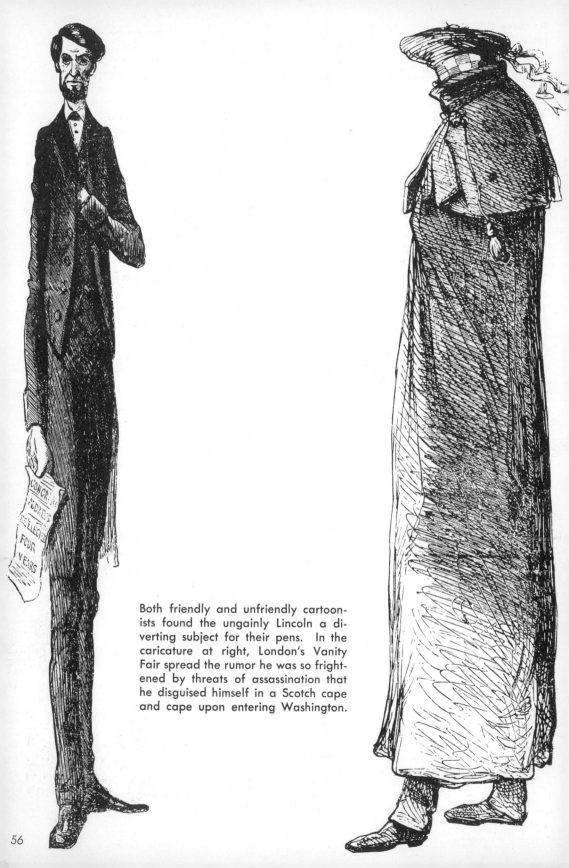

Both friendly and unfriendly cartoonists found the ungainly Lincoln a diverting subject for their pens. In the caricature at right, London's Vanity Fair spread the rumor he was so frightened by threats of assassination that he disguised himself in a Scotch cape and cape upon entering Washington.

As these caricatures show, Lincoln was subjected to brutal vilification. The unsubtle purpose of the cartoon on the right was to give currency to reports that That Man in the White House was of Negro lineage.

In the drawing below, Lincoln is shown with his feet besmirching the Constitution; Satan is providing counsel from a table decorated with Negro gargoyles and cloven feet.

"Loyal Americans", a lithograph by A. K. Kipps, featured members of Lincoln's cabinet and prominent military figures. Young Col. Ephraim Ellsworth (bottom left), an early casualty of the war, was once a clerk in Lincoln's law office.

In May 1862 the Department of Agriculture was established with Isaac Newton (seated in center) as it head. Early officials of the agency surround Mr. Newton.

First home of the newly created Department of Agriculture in Washington, D. C.

In the same year—on May 15, 1862, to be exact—Lincoln signed the far-reaching Homestead Act, authorizing freehold farm tracts of 160 acres to citizens agreeing to make homes on them for not less than five years. The measure had been strongly advocated by the Republican Party from its inception, but pro-slavery sentiment, fearing extension of Northern influence, had blocked passage; Southern secession removed the last remaining obstacle. Acclaimed "the greatest democratic measure of all history", the Homestead law threw open to settlement some 275,000,000 acres, greatly facilitated the development of the west, and substantially contributed to the doubling of the nation's population in the period 1860-1890.

The first man to file a claim under the Homestead Act, Daniel Freeman was the prototype of the thousands who benefited by that law during the 1860s. He staked out his claim at Brownville, Nebraska, while on leave from military duty with the Union forces.

Daniel Freeman, pioneer homesteader.

These western settlers were among the first to take advantage of the liberal Homestead Act.

Land Scrip No. *5291* for "One Quarter Section."

Colleges for Agriculture and Mechanic Arts.

ACT OF CONGRESS, JULY 2, 1862

For State of New York

Whereas, in pursuance of the Act of Congress approved July 2, 1862, entitled "An act donating Public Lands to the several States and Territories which may provide Colleges for the benefit of Agriculture and the Mechanic Arts:*

The State of New York has accepted the Grant provided by the said act, and, under the same, has consequently a legal claim to One Hundred and Ninety Thousand acres, not locatable by the State itself, but liable to transfer, and may be located by the **Assignees** *of said* **state**, *according to assignment, attested by two witnesses, in the form on the back of this instrument; the locations by Assignees in satisfaction of the claim above mentioned, to be made in virtue of a regular Series of Scrip, a part of which is this:*

Land Scrip No. *5291* for "One Quarter Section."

Therefore be it known, That this **SCRIP,** *when duly assigned and attested by two witnesses, under such authority of the said State as the act of the Legislature thereof may designate, may be surrendered at any Land Office of the* UNITED STATES *in satisfaction of a location of "One Quarter of a Section" or for any quantity in one legal subdivision less than "One Quarter Section," where such location is taken in full for "One Quarter Section"—the location to be restricted to* **vacant** *public lands* **subject to entry at private** *sale at $1.25 per acre,* MINERAL LANDS EXCLUDED; *and whilst the aggregate location of all the claims under the said act may be taken in any of the* TERRITORIES *without limitation as to the quantity located in any one of them, yet, in virtue of express limitation in the Statute, "not more than One Million Acres" of the total aggregate Scrip issue under said act can be located within the limits "of any one of the States."*

Given under my hand and seal of the Department of the Interior on the twenty second day of May A. D. 1863, and of the Independence of the United States the Eighty Eighth.

Recorded, Vol. 49 Page 41.

J. M. Edmunds
Commissioner of the General Land Office.

W. T. Otto
Acting Secretary of the Interior.

GOV'T PRINT. OFFICE.

Certificates such as the above transferred land from the federal government to the states under the terms of the Land-Grant College Act approved by Lincoln on July 2, 1862. One of the most important measures ever passed by Congress, this law gave tremendous impetus to democratic education. Popularly known as the Morrill Land-Grant Act after its sponsor, Senator Justin S. Morrill of Vermont, the bill initially assigned to each state, for public college use, some 30,000 acres of federal land for each U.S. Senator and Representative then serving the state. The generous provisions of the law (more than 118,000,000 acres were donated up to 1940) substantially aided existing institutions and made possible the establishment of scores of new ones. Today one out of every five college students is attending a land-grant school.

Secretary of the Treasury Salmon P. Chase conferring with President Lincoln regarding the National Bank Act of 1863, which laid the foundation for the present national banking system. This important measure established safeguards for depositors, initiated uniformity of regulations, and provided for federal supervision and inspection.

The first dollar bill was issued in 1862, when paper money—"greenbacks"—became legal tender for all debts. Above reproduction is by special permission of the U.S. Treasury Department.

Lincoln's frequent visits to the battle areas boosted morale for troops and officers alike. Here he is seen at Antietam with General John McClernand and Allan Pinkerton, founder of U.S. Secret Service.

Reconnaissance balloons provided the Union armies with vital information about Southern troop movements and led directly to the formation of the nation's first military air corps.

The war gave real impetus to the large-scale employment of women as factory and office workers. Thousands joined in the manufacture of munitions (preparing cartridges, for example, as in the scene above) and many entered the federal service (below are Treasury Department clerks departing for the boarding houses they called home).

Above is a representation of a federal charter granted to the Union Pacific Railroad under the provisions of the Pacific Railway Act of July 1, 1862. This legislation, which greatly facilitated westward expansion, authorized transcontinental railroad construction and provided generous Federal government aid for the purpose.

Laying the transcontinental link was frequently interrupted by friction with unfriendly Indian

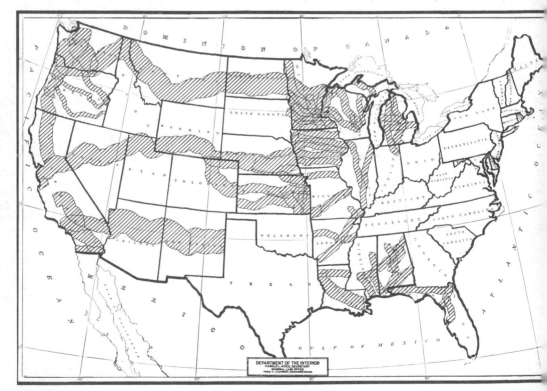

Federal land grants originally made to encourage the construction of railroads are shown
the above Interior Department map. Most of the land was sold to the settlers fairly cheap

The railroads materially helped win the war and unite the country. Quick to recognize the potentialities of this new instrument, General McClellan, a pre-war railroad man, wrote to Lincoln in July 1861: "It can not be ignored that the construction of railroads has introduced a new and very important element into war by the great facilities thus given for concentrating at particular positions large masses of troops from remote sections and by creating new strategic points and lines of operations." In this photo by Mathew Brady a Pinkerton agent is watching a bridge of the Orange and Alexandria Railroad as a train loaded with military supplies is about to depart for the front.

America's first oil boom followed close upon the wheels of railroad progress in the early 1860's. The successful drilling operations of ex-hotel clerk Edwin L. Drake at Titusville, Pennsylvania (above), marked the beginning of the nation's petroleum industry. By 1862 the production of oil in the United States rose to almost a million barrels.

Reading the first draft of the immortal Emancipation Proclamation at a Cabinet meeting on July 22, 1862. Left to right are Secretary of War Stanton, Secretary of the Treasury Chase, President Lincoln, Secretary of the Navy Welles, Secretary of State Seward, Secretary of the Interior Smith, Postmaster General Blair, and Attorney General Bates. The second draft, made public on September 22, warned that its terms would apply to all states still in rebellion at the end of the year. The final version went into effect on January 1, 1863.

As I would not be a slave, so I would not be a master. This expresses my idea of democracy — Whatever differs from this, to the extent of the difference, is no democracy —

A. Lincoln —

The conviction behind these earlier memorable words inspired the historic Proclamation.

By the President of the United States of America:

A Proclamation.

Whereas, on the twenty-second day of September, in the year of our Lord one thousand eight hundred and sixty-two, a proclamation was issued by the President of the United States, containing, among other things, the following, to wit:

"That on the first day of January, in the "year of our Lord one thousand eight hundred "and sixty-three, all persons held as slaves within "any State or designated part of a State, the people "whereof shall then be in rebellion against the "United States, shall be then, thenceforward, and "forever free; and the Executive Government of the "United States, including the military and naval "authority thereof, will recognize and maintain "the freedom of such persons, and will do no act "or acts to repress such persons, or any of them, "in any efforts they may make for their actual "freedom.

"That the Executive will, on the first day

One of the greatest landmarks of world history, the Proclamation liberated three and a half million slaves and changed the status of nearly one-eighth of the inhabitants of the United States from that of chattels who could be bought and sold in the auction market to that of men and women endowed with the right to "life, liberty, and the pursuit of happiness."

FOR PRESIDENT,

Abraham Lincoln
OF ILLINOIS.

FOR VICE PRESIDENT,

Andrew Johnson
OF TENNESSEE.

Despite strong opposition from "Radical" Republicans and widespread disappointment over Northern losses, Lincoln was renominated in 1864 on a "Union" ticket designed to attract the support of loyal Democrats. By way of encouraging national unity sentiment among wavering Southerners, Andrew Johnson, a former Governor of the border state of Tennessee, was chosen Lincoln's running mate.

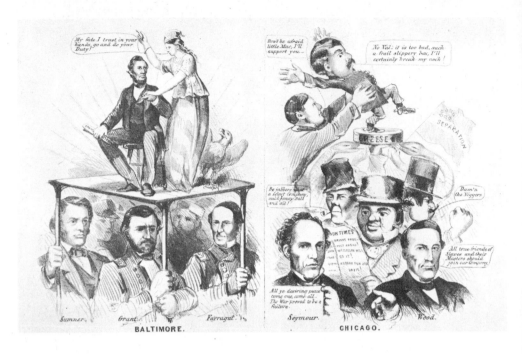

The artists of these campaign items left little doubt as to their opinions. In the lithograph above, General George McClellan, the Democratic candidate, is represented as a puppet of distinctly disreputable elements. In the cartoon below, McClellan is shown as a slavery advocate shaking hands with Jefferson Davis, President of the Confederacy.

UNION AND LIBERTY! AND UNION AND SLAVERY!

A lithograph entitled "A Little Game of Bagatelle, Between Old Abe the Rail Splitter and little Mac the Gunboat General."

Gulliver Abe Lincoln sleeps quite calmly while political pygmies of 1864 take his measure critical

This, in effect, would be the inevitable consequence of McClellan's election, Thomas Nast warne

Cheers rang out in Congress when the Thirteenth Amendment, the last great achievement of Lincoln's administration, was approved January 31, 1865. Its words were plain and clear; "neither slavery nor involuntary servitude, except as punishment for a crime, whereof the party shall have been duly convicted, shall exist within the United States or any place subject to their jurisdiction." The elated House of Representatives "adjourned in honor of the immortal and sublime event." After ratification by three fourths of the states, the amendment went into effect on December 18, 1865.

Welcoming the three Confederate Commissioners—Alexander H. Stephens, John A. Campbell, and Robert M. T. Hunter—who discussed possible peace terms with Lincoln and Secretary of State Seward at Fort Monroe late in January of 1865. Although the meeting did not result in cessation of hostilities, it paved the way to the end of the war several months later.

When Lincoln took the oath of office for the second time on March 4, 1865, the war was almost over. To the crowds gathered in front of the Capitol he addressed immortal words: "With malice toward none, with charity for all, with firmness in the right as God gives us to see the right, let us strive on to finish the work we are in, to bind up the nation's wounds, to care for him who shall have borne the battle and for his widow and his orphan, to do all which may achieve and cherish a just and lasting peace among ourselves and with all nations."

Indian chiefs who brought complaints to the White House found the President sympathetic.

More than six thousand persons reportedly shook hands with Lincoln at a "Grand Reception" held on the evening of his second inauguration; standing at his right is Vice President Johnson.

Mending the nation with the help of Tailor Johnson was considered Lincoln's major objective.

Lincoln is shown inviting the Southern states to take their seats again at the national table.

"All Seems Well With Us." When this drawing was prepared for Harper's Weekly, Lincoln had just received news of the surrender of Lee's army at Appomatox on April 9th and the end of the war was expected momentarily, but when the magazine reached its readers Lincoln was dead.

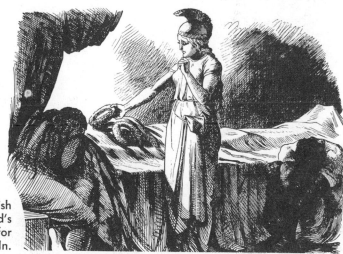

In this representation of British grief, the editors of England's Punch offered some atonement for their earlier treatment of Lincoln.

Lincoln's funeral bier passing through Chicago on the long, sad journey to Springfield.

Elected with Lincoln on the Republican sponsored Union ticket of 1864, Johnson was handicapped from the outset of his administration because of his previous status as a Democrat. His earliest occupation was that of an apprentice to a tailor; he set up his own shop while still in his teens. With the help of his young wife he learned to read and participated in Tennessee politics. Before becoming Vice President he had been Alderman, Mayor, state legislator, member of the House of Representatives (1843-53), Governor of Tennessee (1853-57), and U.S. Senator (1857-62). Loyal to the Union during the Civil War, he was appointed Military Governor of Tennessee and rose to the rank of Brigadier General. At right is his wife.

The modest birthplace of Andrew Johnson in Raleigh, North Carolina. Left fatherless when he was four years old, he went to work when he was ten.

In this Greenville, Tennessee, tailor shop, Johnson deftly combined cutting and sewing with politics. Here his wife taught him to read in his spare time.

An interior view of Johnson's shop as now maintained by the National Park Service.

Johnson succeeded to the Presidency on April 15, 1865, several hours after Lincoln's death. The oath of office was administered by Chief Justice Salmon P. Chase, former Secretary of the Treasury.

The largest military parade in American history took place on May 23 and 24, 1865, when victorious Union troops marched past President Johnson's reviewing stand near the White House.

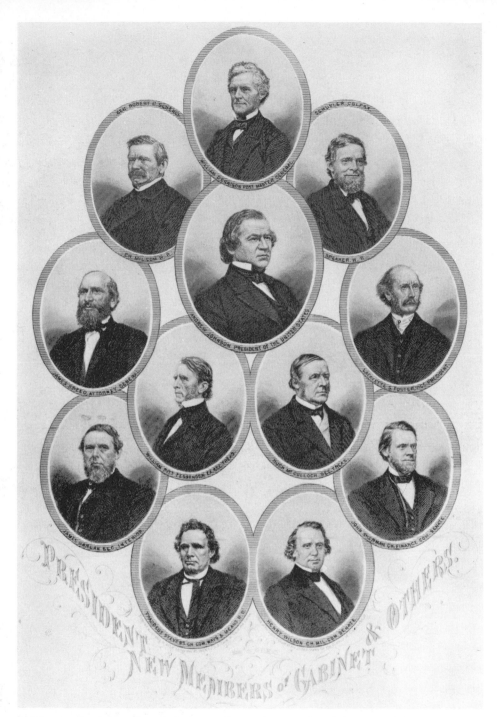

A lithograph of President Johnson with members of his Cabinet and key figures of Congress. Reading clockwise from the top are Postmaster General William Dennison, Rep. Schuyler Colfax, Senator Lafayette Foster, Senator John Sherman, Senator Henry Wilson, Rep. Thaddeus Stevens, Secretary of Interior James Harlan, Attorney General James Speed, and Rep. Robert Schenck. Beneath Johnson are William Fessenden (left), and his successor as Secretary of the Treasury, Hugh McCulloch.

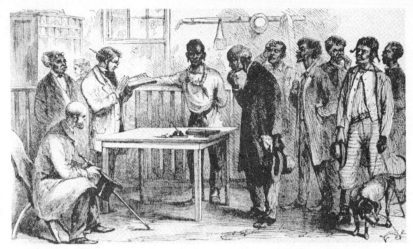

Assisting ex-slaves was the difficult job of the new Freedmen's Bureau.

More than $5,000,000 was spent on special school facilities for Negroes.

The needy received rations and medical aid on a large scale.

87

President Johnson pardoning Confederates at the White House. A proclamation of amnesty, issued on May 29, 1865, seemed ill-advised to some Northerners. Sharp differences between Johnson and Congress over reconstruction policies inspired the lithograph reproduced below.

This intemperate caricature by Thomas Nast epitomized the views of Johnson's critics toward his policies and those of Secretary of State William H. Seward (bottom inset).

Johnson's critics contended that his "soft" reconstruction policy encouraged the Ku Klux Klan movement. In the lawlessness which became widespread they saw evidence of the incorrigibility of the South. Originally founded as an innocent fraternal organization, the KKK was soon twisted into a terroristic movement. Its masked and hooded members maimed and killed many of their victims.

Johnson's supporters, on the other hand, felt that trouble-making carpetbaggers and harsh treatment of the South meted out in Congressional measures passed over Presidential vetoes were chiefly responsible for the growth of the Ku Klux Klan. An early purpose of the organization, it was noted, was to protect Southern whites from humiliation by Negroes and unfair treatment by Northern agents.

When Johnson found himself stymied by Congress, he made a direct appeal for popular support.

His policies were espoused at "Arm-in-Arm" meetings attended by many Civil War veterans.

The most outstanding member of Johnson's Cabinet, Secretary of State William H. Seward, arranged for the purchase of Alaska from Russia at a cost of about two cents an acre —an action widely criticized as a waste of the taxpayers' money. A dominant personality in the Republican Party, he almost received the Presidential nomination in 1860.

Consummation of the Alaska deal was reached at 4 a.m. on March 30, 1867, in Seward's office
In the above painting of the event, Seward is seated at the left and Russia's Minister to the U.S
is pointing at the location of the newly acquired territory.   Many Americans were unimpressed

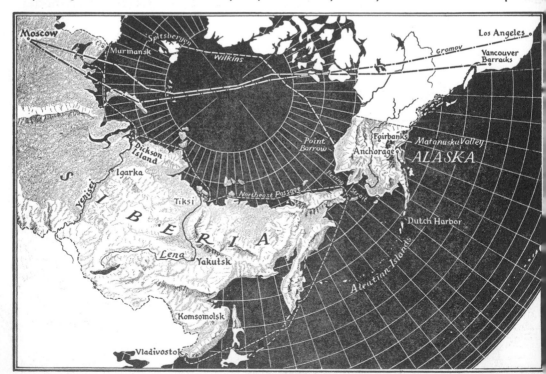

The U.S. acquired immense natural resources and a strategic bastion for Pacific defense.

Johnson's spectacular impeachment trial in the Senate chamber climaxed a long series of bitter conflicts with Congress. Major issue at the trial was the propriety of Johnson's dismissal of Edwin Stanton as Secretary of War without Senate sanction.   Impeachment was averted by one vote.

"The Smelling Committee", a lithograph deriding the instigators of the impeachment action.

An important factor in winning the Civil War and uniting the nation during Johnson's administration was electric telegraphy. Early in the 1860's the western states became a more closely integrated part of the nation through the construction of telegraph lines between the Missouri River and California under government auspices. During the war, Union armies used telegraphy for the first time in military history. By the close of the 1860's the principal cities of the nation were closely bound together by telegraph communication. In 1866 Cyrus W. Field completed the laying of the trans-Atlantic cable providing submarine telegraphy between the new and old worlds.

Laying the trans-Atlantic cable from the "Great Eastern".

The tall man silhouetted against the window near the center is Cyrus W. Field. He and his associates are shown awaiting the reply to the first message transmitted via the Atlantic cable

The joining of the tracks of the Union Pacific Railroad with those of the Central Pacific line on May 10, 1869, at Promontory, Utah, marked the most important accomplishment under the terms of the Pacific Railway Act of July 1, 1862.   East and West were united firmly by rails of steel.

To arouse interest in western settlement, the Union Pacific outfitted a special photographic car.

Homes for the Industrious!

— IN THE —

GARDEN STATE OF THE WEST.

THE ILLINOIS CENTRAL RAILROAD CO., HAVE FOR SALE

1,200,000 ACRES OF RICH FARMING LANDS,

In Tracts of Forty Acres and upward, on Long Credit and at Low Prices.

MECHANICS, FARMERS AND WORKING MEN.

THE attention of the enterprising and industrious portion of the community is directed to the following statements and liberal inducements offered them by the

ILLINOIS CENTRAL RAILROAD COMPANY.

which, as they will perceive, will enable them by proper energy, perseverance and industry, to provide comfortable homes for themselves and families, with, comparatively speaking, very little capital.

LANDS OF ILLINOIS.

No State in the Valley of the Mississippi offers so great an inducement as the State of Illinois. There is no portion of the world where all the conditions of climate and soil so admirably combine to produce those two great staples, CORN and WHEAT, as the Prairies of Illinois.

THE SOUTHERN PART

of the State lies within the zone of the cotton regions, while the soil is admirably adapted to the growth of tobacco and hemp; and the wheat is worth from fifteen to twenty cents more per bushel than that raised further north.

RICH ROLLING PRAIRIE LANDS.

The deep rich loam of the prairies is cultivated with such wonderful facility that the farmers of the Eastern and Middle States are moving to Illinois in great numbers. The area of Illinois is about equal to that of England, and the soil is so rich that it will support twenty millions of people.

EASTERN AND SOUTHERN MARKETS.

These lands are contiguous to a railroad 700 miles in length, which connects with other roads and navigable lakes and rivers, thus affording an unbroken communication with the Eastern and Southern markets.

APPLICATION OF CAPITAL.

Thus far, capital and labor have been applied to developing the soil; the great resources of the State in coal and iron are almost untouched. The invariable rule that the mechanical arts flourish best where food and fuel are cheapest, will follow at an early day in Illinois, and in the course of the next ten years the natural laws and necessities of the case warrant the belief that at least five hundred thousand people will be engaged in the State of Illinois in various manufacturing pursuits.

RAILROAD SYSTEM OF ILLINOIS.

Over $100,000,000 of private capital have been expended on the railways of Illinois. Inasmuch as part of the income from several these works, with a valuable public fund in lands, go to diminish the State expenses, the TAXES ARE LIGHT, and must consequently every day decrease.

THE STATE DEBT.

The State Debt is only $10,105,398, 14, and within the last three years has been reduced $2,959,746 80, and we may reasonably expect that in ten years it will become extinct.

Pamphlets descriptive of the lands, soil, climate, productions, prices and terms of payment, can be had on application to

PRESENT POPULATION,

The State is rapidly filling up with population; 868,025 persons having been added since 1850, making the present population 1,723,663, a ratio of 102 per cent. in ten years.

AGRICULTURAL PRODUCTS.

The Agricultural products of Illinois are greater than those of any other State. The products sent out during the past year exceeded 1,500,000 tons. The wheat crop of 1860 approaches 35,000,000 bushels, while the corn crop yields not less than 140,000,000 bushels.

FERTILITY OF THE SOIL.

Nowhere can the industrious farmer secure such immediate results for his labor as upon these prairie soils, they being composed of a deep rich loam, the fertility of which, is unsurpassed by any on the globe.

TO ACTUAL CULTIVATORS.

Since 1854, the company have sold 1 300,000 acres. They sell only to actual cultivators, and every contract contains an agreement to cultivate. The road has been constructed thro' these lands at an expense of $30,000,000. In 1850 the population of the forty-nine counties through which it passes was only 335,598; since which 479,293 have been added, making the whole population 814,891, a gain of 143 per cent.

EVIDENCES OF PROSPERITY.

As an evidence of the thrift of the people, it may be stated that 600,000 tons of freight, including 8,600,000 bushels of grain, and 250,000 barrels of flour, were forwarded over the line last year

EDUCATION.

Mechanics and workingmen will find the free school system encouraged by the State, and endowed with a large revenue for the support of schools. Their children can live in sight of the church and schoolhouse and grow with the prosperity of the leading State in the Great Western Empire.

PRICES AND TERMS OF PAYMENT.

The prices of these lands vary from $6 to $25 per acre according to location, quality, &c. First-class farming lands sell for about $10 or $12 per acre; and the relative expense of subduing prairie land as compared with wood lands is in the ratio of 1 to 10 in favor of the former. The terms of sale for the bulk of these lands will be

One Year's Interest in advance,

at six per ct. per annum, and six interest notes at six per ct. payable respectively in one, two, three, four, five and six years from date of sale; and four notes for principal, payable in four, five, six and seven years from date of sale; the contract stipulating that one-tenth of the tract purchased shall be fenced and cultivated, each and every year, for five years from date of sale, so that at the end of five years, one-half shall be fenced and under cultivation.

Twenty Per Cent. will be deducted

from the valuation for cash, except the same should be at six dollars per acre, when the cash price will be five dollars.

J. W. FOSTER, Land Commissioner, Chicago, Illinois.

For the names of the Towns, Villages and Cities situated upon the Illinois Central Railroad see pages 188, 189, 190, APPLETON'S RAILWAY GUIDE.

Advertisements such as the above lured easterners westward. Assisted by government aid, the railroads sold land near their tracks at low rates in order to encourage settlement. Note train conveniences on opposite page.

99

As settlers pushed westward, conflicts with unfriendly
Indians necessitated protection by federal troops.

Northern and southern veterans of the Civil War
joined hands in carving new states out of the prairies.

Land agents of Johnson's administration literally did a land office business in helping settlers obtain Homestead Act benefits. The photo below was taken in Nebraska in 1869.

Harvesting grain on a Civil War battlefield presaged better days.

Celebrating Independence Day — an engraving in Harper's Weekly.

Traffic on the Mississippi was so heavy that collisions were frequent.

Left: Grant's
birthplace

Ulysses S. Grant was born on April 27,
1822, at Point Pleasant, Ohio. Upon
his admission to West Point in 1839, he
registered under his baptismal name,
Ulysses Hiram Grant, but he accepted
Ulysses Simpson Grant as his new
name when he discovered that his
Congressman had so listed him. After
his graduation he served in the Mexi-
can War and was brevetted Captain
for gallantry. In 1854 he resigned
from the Army to enter private business; unsuccessful in his enterprises, he
became a clerk in his father's leather
store in Galena, Illinois, and was earning $800 a year when he answered
Lincoln's call for volunteers in 1861.

Miss Julia T. Dent of St. Louis became
Mrs. Grant on August 22, 1848.

Early in 1864 Lincoln raised Grant to the rank of Lieutenant General and gave him supreme command of the Northern armies. In forcing Lee's surrender at Appomattox on April 9, 1865, he brought the Civil War to a close and won the Union's gratitude.

The only known photograph of the Grant family prior to 1865. With General and Mrs. Grant are their children (left to right): Nellie, Jessie, Frederick, and U. S. Grant, Jr.

This unusual picture includes Grant during a visit to the Bonanza Mine in Nevada. From left to right are John Mackay, Mrs. M. G. Gillette, U.S. Grant, Jr., Mrs. Ulysses S. Grant, Grant, Mrs. James G. Fair, Governor J. H. Kinkhead of Nevada, and James G. Fair. The owner of the mine, Mackay was also the founder of the Postal Telegraph System. Mrs. Fair was the mother of Mrs. William K. Vanderbilt. The photo was taken in 1879.

THE LEADER AND HIS BATTLES

CAPTURE OF FORT DONELSON.
FEBRUARY 16th, 1862.

BATTLE AT PITTSBURG LANDING,
APRIL 6th, 1862.

GEN. PEMBERTON SURRENDERS VICKSBURG TO GEN. GRANT.
JULY 4th, 1863.

SURRENDER OF GENERAL LEE.
APRIL 9th, 1865.

ULYSSES S. GRANT,
LIEUTENANT-GENERAL, U. S. A.

Grant's tremendous popularity at the end of the Civil War made his candidacy for President almost inevitable. His gallantry toward General Robert E. Lee in the hour of victory aroused regard of the North and respect of the South. "Grant showed many admirable and lovable traits," wrote historian John Fiske. "There was a charming side to his trustful simplicity. He abounded in kindness and generosity, and if there was anything especially difficult for him to endure, it was the sight of human suffering, as was shown on the night at Shiloh, where he lay out of doors in the icy rain rather than stay in a comfortable room where the surgeons were at work. His good sense was strong, as well as his sense of justice, and these qualities stood him in good service as President . . . Altogether, in spite of some shortcomings, Grant was a massive, noble, and lovable personality, well fit to be remembered as one of the heroes of a great nation."

Grant with his family in 1868 (left to right): Jessie, Nellie, U. S. Grant, Jr., Frederick, Mrs. Grant, and General Grant. In his reminiscences about his father, Frederick wrote: "In private and in public life he was a plain, dignified, undemonstrative man, with a quiet, self-controlled manner which never left him, showing a consideration in all his actions and words towards others which I have never seen equalled . . . My father was a strict disciplinarian with his children, although most kind and gentle, and always thoughtful of our happiness. While it became necessary on a few occasions to severely punish some of us, his unusual method of correction was to show disapproval of our action by his manner and quiet words. This was far more effective with us than scoldings or whippings . . . He was loyal to his family, to his friends and to his country."

Grant's nomination by Representative John A. Logan was approved by unanimous vote on the first ballot of the Republican convention held in Chicago in the summer of 1868.

GEN. U.S. GRANT FOR PRESIDENT.

NATIONAL UNION REPUBLICAN CANDIDATES

HON. SCHUYLER COLFAX FOR VICE PRESIDENT.

Their selection was greeted enthusiastically throughout the North and in the border states. While Grant took comparatively little part in the campaign, Colfax spoke often.

These comparisons of the wartime records of Grant and Horatio Seymour, the Democratic candidate, contributed to the defeat of the latter. The essential idea of both cartoons is that while Grant had saved the Union, Seymour had undermined it by supporting "Copperhead" sabotage

The "Great Race for the Presidential Sweepstakes Between the Western War Horse, U. S. Grant, and the Manhattan Donkey" was Nasby's title for the above cartoon. In the caricature below, New York's Governor Hoffman, dressed in Tammany regalia, is seen presenting Seymour and his running mate, Frank P. Blair, for "tanning". In his youth Grant had been a leather tanner.

"Vote As You Shot" appealed to Union veterans and Grant admirers.

In this campaign cartoon Thomas Nast again came to the support of the Repub

Early state election returns plunged Seymour into "a sea of troubles".

...rty highly effectively; "The Boys in Blue and the Boys in Grey" was the title he gave it.

Grant came to the Presidency amid stupendous enthusiasm. In taking the oath of office on March 4, 1869, he declared: "The young men of the country—those who from their age must be its rulers twenty-five years hence—have a peculiar interest in maintaining the national honor. A moment's reflection as to what will be our commanding influence among the nations of the earth in their day, if they are only true to themselves, should inspire them with national pride. All divisions—geographical, political, religious—can join in the common sentiment. How the public debt is to be paid or specie payment resumed is not so important as that a plan should be adopted and acquiesced in ... In regard to foreign policy, I would deal with nations as equitable law requires individuals to deal with each other, and I would protect the law-abiding citizen, whether of native or foreign birth, wherever his rights are jeopardized or the flag of our country floats. I would respect the rights of all nations, expecting equal respect for our own."

Grant and his Cabinet in 1869 (left to right): Jacob D. Cox, Secretary of the Interior; Hamilton Fish, Secretary of State; John A. Rawlins, Secretary of War; John A. Creswell, Postmaster General; President Grant; George S. Boutwell, Secretary of the Treasury; Adolph E. Borie, Secretary of the Navy; Ebenezer R. Hoar, Attorney General.

Garrulous, amiable Schuyler Colfax of Indiana, the new Vice President, was the Speaker of the House of Representatives when he was chosen Grant's running mate.

Many Northerners advocated the reconstruction views suggested by the artist of this lithograph. During Grant's first administration the rights guaranteed to Negroes by the Fourteenth and Fifteenth Amendments to the Constitution were enforced by supplementary legislation.

A friendly, bluff man, Grant found it difficult to turn away favor seekers he knew personally.

When financial panic hit the business world in the summer of 1869 because the price of gold had been forced sky high by unscrupulous speculators, Grant prevented disruption of the nation's currency structure by releasing government gold reserves.

Much of the blame for "Black Friday" was placed on Grant's doorstep by Democrats because he had once dined with Jay Gould, James Fisk and others who cornered the gold market with the help of Treasury official Daniel Butterfield.

Pandemonium broke out on Wall Street during "Black Friday".

Led by John W. Powell, this party explored western resources for the government in 1868-1870.

Criticism of Grant's first administration evoked this defense in Harper's Weekly

Settlement of a whole series of troublesome questions between Great Britain and the United States, a major achievement of Grant's first administration, was negotiated by Secretary of State Hamilton Fish (seen at right with Grant). Under the terms of the Treaty of Washington signed in 1871, England paid $15,500,000 to the U.S. for damages by the "Alabama", a British vessel sold to the Confederates during the Civil War. Claims were arbitrated by representatives of the United States, Great Britain, Switzerland, Brazil, and Italy who met in Geneva. Also settled were disputes pertaining to the southern boundary of Canada and fishery rights in adjoining waters. Anglo-American relations improved markedly in subsequent years.

The apple of discord between the United States and Britain was shattered by John Bull's $15,500,000 arrow. Looking on are the monarchs of Europe (astride horses) and members of the Geneva tribunal (seated on the platform). The Treaty of Washington, according to historian Allan Nevins, effected "the first really great international arbitration of modern times."

Civil service reforms instituted by Grant in 1871 were not altogether to the liking of Horace Greeley, Carl Schurz and other Republican critics.

A lithograph commemorating the passage in 1868 of the eight-hour law for government workers. In 1873 women employed by federal agencies became eligible for equal pay for equal work; a significant precedent was set.

Cheers rang out as Grant was unanimously renominated at the Philadelphia convention of 1872.

"Wildest excitement" followed the nominating speech, according to John Tweedy. "The spacious academy was crowded with thousands of spectators in every part, and on the stage, in the parquet, and in tier upon tier of galleries, arose deafening prolonged, tremendous cheers, swelling from pit to dome. A perfect wilderness of hats, caps, and handkerchiefs waved to and fro in a surging mass . . . The band appeared to catch the prevailing enthusiasm and waved their instruments as though they had been flags . . . they struck up 'Hail to the Chief'. As the majestic stream of music came flooating down from the balcony, a life-size equestrian portrait of General Grant came down, as if by magic, filling the entire space of the back scene, and the enthusiasm knew no bounds."

As maps at right show, the nation had changed markedly since 1850s

THE WORKING·MAN'S BANNER.

FOR PRESIDENT. **FOR VICE-PRESIDENT.**

TANNERY

ULYSSES S. GRANT
"The Galena Tanner"

HENRY WILSON
"The Natick Shoemaker"

Senator Henry Wilson of Massachusetts was evidently given the Vice Presidential nomination in place of Schuyler Colfax because the latter had Presidential aspirations which displeased Grant. Almost wholly self-educated, Wilson was a shoemaker's apprentice in his youth. His original name, Jeremiah Jones Colbath, was changed to Henry Wilson in 1833. During the late 1850's he helped organize the Massachusetts Republican Party.

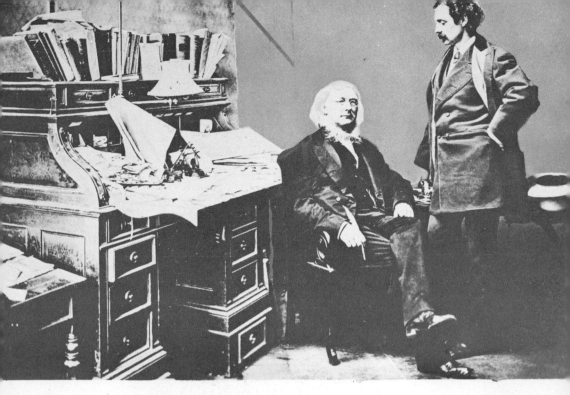

Editor Horace Greeley (seated above), Presidential nominee of the Liberal Republican Party of 1872, represented elements opposed to Grant's nomination and favoring less severe treatment of the South. While their platform was somewhat similar to that of the Republican Party proper, they differed sharply on reconstruction policies. To some of Greeley's admirers it seemed that he had put himself and his paper, the New York Tribune, out on an untenable limb.

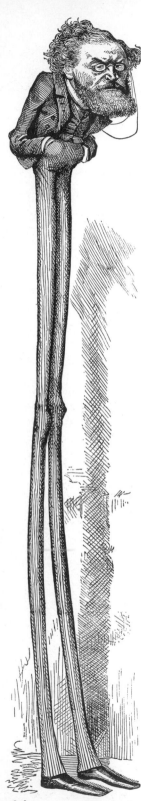

Some considered Greeley a Trojan horse of the Democratic Party because he was a candidate for President with Democratic support.

In the opinion of Thomas Nast, these dissident Senators—Carl Schur Reuben Fenton, Lyman Trumbull, Charles Sumner, and Andrew Tipt —plotted to supplant the Republican Party with the Liberal Repub can Party. Greeley is in the background at the left.

Schurz was Greeley's "tower of strength".

They were the unsuccessful standard bearers of the short-lived Liberal Republican Party. Although their ticket was backed by many Democrats, they carried only six states—all Southern. Grant was returned to office with a popular majority three times greater than that of 1868; he received 272 electoral votes to 63 for opposition candidates.

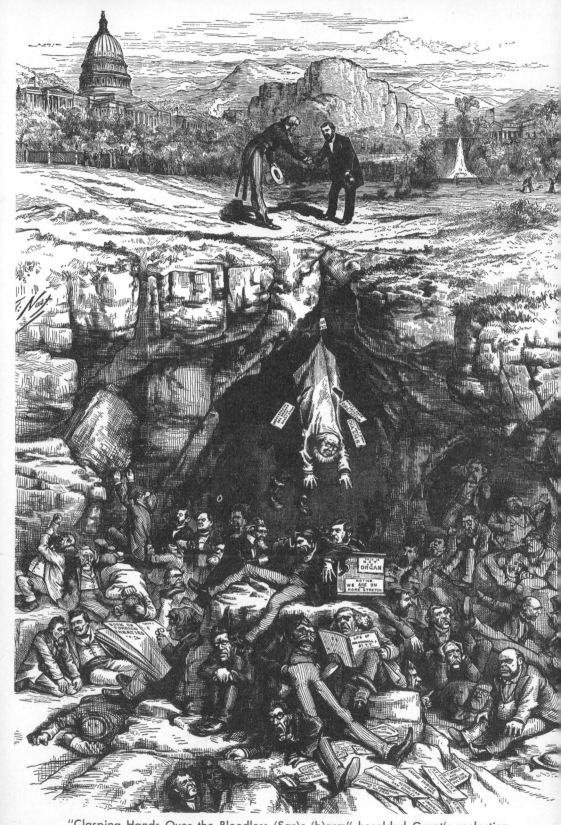

"Clasping Hands Over the Bloodless (Sar)c (h)asm" heralded Grant's reelection.

erpreting his reelec-
n as a complete vin-
cation of his first ad-
inistration, Grant de-
ared in his inaugural
dress of March 4,
73: "I have been the
bject of abuse and
nder scarcely ever
qualed in political his-
ry, which today I feel
at I can afford to dis-
gard in view of your
rdict." Toward the
ose of his speech he
dded prophetically: "It
my firm conviction
at the civilized world
tending toward re-
blicanism or govern-
ent by the people
rough their chosen
presentatives, a n d
at our own great Re-
blic is destined to be
e guiding star . . ."

The coldest of inaugural days, March 4, 1873, was long remembered.

Despite the zero weather, there was lively dancing and gaiety at the Inaugural Ball.

Grant's second term had just begun when the failure of Wall Street's powerful Jay Cooke and Company caused a panic which paralyzed business throughout the country.

At left is a contemporary print of the excitement observed in front of Cooke headquarters in New York.

"BUTLERISM"

BUTLER BOTTLED AGAIN.

VETO

PRESIDENT GRANT WILL NOT VETO THE FINANCE BILL BEN BUTLER

In vetoing Rep. Benjamin Butler's Inflation Bill of 1874, Grant held steadfast to a sound money policy although it was politically inexpedient to do so. His "bottling up of Butler" aroused Congressional indignation but averted depreciation of the nation's currency. The Resumption Act of 1875, passed at Grant's insistence, increased the value of U.S. currency and improved the government's credit; it made paper money redeemable in coin of the realm beginning 1879.

Predominantly Republican, most Senate members pictured above gave Grant's second administration a landslide victory

The elephant as the Republican symbol made its first appearance in the above cartoon by Thomas Nast in Harper's Weekly, November 7, 1874; it it shown being stampeded by lesser political animals into a pit labelled "Southern Claims and Chaos". Escape from the pit, it seemed to Nast, was subsequently made possible by Grant's repudiation of third-term aspirations (below).

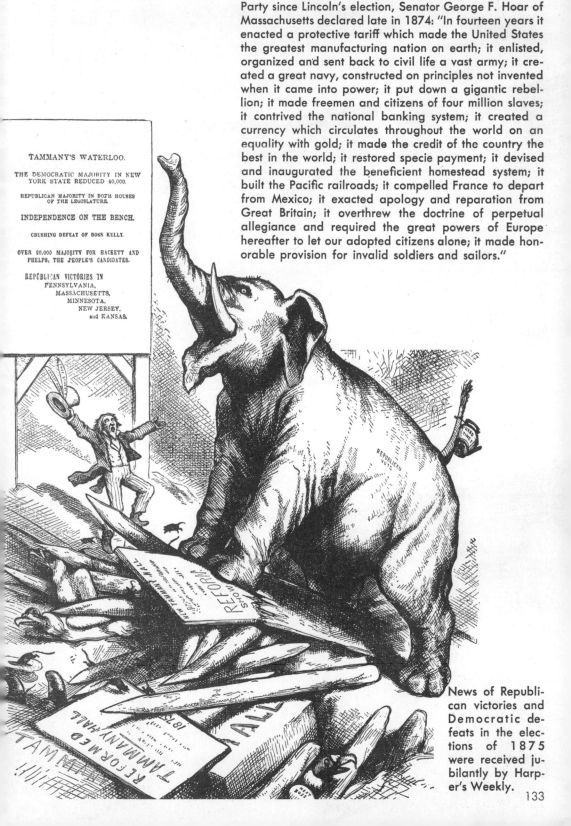

In reviewing the accomplishments of the Republican Party since Lincoln's election, Senator George F. Hoar of Massachusetts declared late in 1874: "In fourteen years it enacted a protective tariff which made the United States the greatest manufacturing nation on earth; it enlisted, organized and sent back to civil life a vast army; it created a great navy, constructed on principles not invented when it came into power; it put down a gigantic rebellion; it made freemen and citizens of four million slaves; it contrived the national banking system; it created a currency which circulates throughout the world on an equality with gold; it made the credit of the country the best in the world; it restored specie payment; it devised and inaugurated the beneficent homestead system; it built the Pacific railroads; it compelled France to depart from Mexico; it exacted apology and reparation from Great Britain; it overthrew the doctrine of perpetual allegiance and required the great powers of Europe hereafter to let our adopted citizens alone; it made honorable provision for invalid soldiers and sailors."

TAMMANY'S WATERLOO.

THE DEMOCRATIC MAJORITY IN NEW YORK STATE REDUCED 40,000.

REPUBLICAN MAJORITY IN BOTH HOUSES OF THE LEGISLATURE.

INDEPENDENCE ON THE BENCH.

CRUSHING DEFEAT OF BOSS KELLY.

OVER 20,000 MAJORITY FOR HACKETT AND PHELPS, THE PEOPLE'S CANDIDATES.

REPUBLICAN VICTORIES IN
PENNSYLVANIA,
MASSACHUSETTS,
MINNESOTA,
NEW JERSEY,
and KANSAS.

News of Republican victories and Democratic defeats in the elections of 1875 were received jubilantly by Harper's Weekly.

133

When charges of misconduct forced Secretary [of] War William F. Belknap (right) to resign in 18[76] Grant was both disappointed and embarrass[ed].

To cartoonist Thomas Nas[t it] seemed that Grant was m[ade] a scapegoat by his politi[cal] enemies. "The Crowning [In-]sult to Him Who Occupies [the] Presidential Chair" was [the] title of this drawing. Des[pite] efforts to associate him w[ith] the irregularities that mar[ked] his second administrati[on,] Grant's personal integrity w[as] in no way involved.

Russian expansion toward the Pacific was deftly countered by American moves in that area. In 1875 Secretary of State Hamilton Fish entered into a reciprocity treaty with Hawaii (then named the Sandwich Isles) whereby sugar and other native commodities were admitted to the U.S. free of tariffs in return for Hawaiian admission of American products and assurance that none of the islands would be sold or traded to any other country.

Immigration rose to a million a year during the 1870's. This print appeared in Harper's Weekly.

135

Bloodiest conflict of the war with hosti
Sioux and Cheyenne Indians was the batt
of the Little Bighorn River on June 25-2
1876. It was in this encounter that Custer an
a battalion of 231 men made their hero
"last stand." They were completely ann
hilated in a surprise attack by an overwhelm
ing force of redmen with modern weapon

Winning of the west during Grant's second administration was substantially advanced by Major
General George A. Custer. A dashing figure of
a man, he was greatly admired for his courage.

Disregarding the terms of the Fort Laram
Treaty of 1868, Chief Sitting Bull (abov
prevailed upon Sioux and other Indians
resist Custer and his troops in Montana.

Top: Crow Indian scouts who served under Custer are seen visiting the spot on which he and his men were slaughtered.

Bottom: Custer with several of the scouts who accompanied him during the Yellowstone expedition of 1873. At his right is "Bloody Knife", who lost his life in the battle preceding Custer's "last stand".

The hundredth birthday of the nation was marked by this lithograph in 18

America took stock of its material and cultural progress with pride and wonder.

At Philadelphia's Centennial Exposition the nation saw its achievements in grandiose display. Accompanied by the Emperor of Brazil, President Grant officially opened the fair by setting in motion the huge Corliss steam engine standing in the center of Machinery Hall. In but a few generations, it was plainly evident in every exhibit, the United States had become a truly great nation. The past was memorable, the present exciting, the future dazzling.

The exhibits of Horticultural Hall confirmed that the United States was rapidly becoming the world's richest and most productive source of food.

An air conditioning device aroused both indignation and admiration.

The typewriter symbolized a new era for women and a revolution in business communication.

On Sundays and holidays the nation enjoyed the fruits of peace and prosperity with democratic gusto.

Coming into office under a cloud, Rutherford Birchard Hayes (seen above with his wife Lucy) was not only handicapped by doubts as to the validity of his election as President in 1876, but also by Democratic control of the House of Representatives throughout his administration and by a Democratic Senate for two years. Yet comparatively few occupants of the White House fulfilled their responsibilities more constructively than he. A native of Delaware, Ohio (he was born there on October 4, 1822), Hayes was educated in the public schools, attended Kenyon College, studied law at Harvard, and was admitted to the Cincinnati bar in his early twenties. Upon the outbreak of the Civil War he joined the Union forces as a volunteer. Although wounded four times, he remained in the Army almost up to the end of the conflict; when he was mustered out he was a Major General. In 1865 he was sent to the House of Representatives and two years later he was elected Governor of Ohio, an office he held for three terms. Opposition to a third term for Ulysses S. Grant and to the nomination of James Gillespie Blaine at the 1876 convention resulted in his selection as a compromise dark horse candidate for the Presidency.

Hayes' birthplace in Delaware, Ohio; a monument now marks the spot.

"Rud" and Lucy Webb Hayes shortly after their wedding in 1852.

Above is a Mathew Brady photograph of President Hayes with two of his sons. Below is the Hayes homestead adjoining the Hayes Memorial Library in Fremont, Ohio.

LIBERTY AND UNION

GOV. RUTHERFORD B. HAYES,

HON. WM. A. WHEELER

FOR PRESIDENT.

FOR VICE-PRESIDENT.

GRAND NATIONAL REPUBLICAN BANNER.

A Currier and Ives lithograph issued in honor of the nomination of Hayes and Wheeler by the Republican convention held in Cincinnati in June 1876. As the author of the "Wheeler Compromise" which brought an end to political disturbances in Louisiana, William A. Wheeler, a New York Congressman, attracted much attention in 1875.

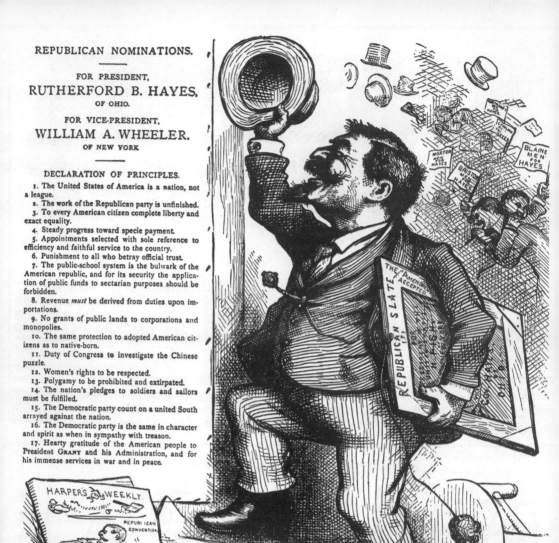

The platform on which Hayes was nominated evoked this cartoon by Thomas Nast in which he depicted himself waving his hat. In view of the scandals which had marred Grant's second administration, the following plank was considered noteworthy: "We rejoice in the quickened conscience of the people concerning political affairs, and will hold all public officers to a rigid responsibility, and engage that the prosecution and punishment of all who betray official trusts shall be swift, thorough, and unsparing." Concerning polygamy, a Mormon practice which had aroused widespread indignation, the platform took the position that Congress should "prohibit and extirpate . . . that relic of barbarism." On women's rights, the platform stated: "The Republican Party recognizes with its approval the substantial advances recently made toward the establishment of equal rights for women by the many important amendments effected by Republican legislatures in the laws which concern the personal and property relations of wives, mothers, and widows, and by the appointment and election of women to . . . public trusts. The honest demands of this class of citizens for additional rights, privileges, and immunities should be treated with respectful consideration."

148

DEMOCRATS

'PUT UP'

OR

SHUT UP

I Want to BET From

$100 to $500!

THAT R. B. HAYES

Will be elected President of the United States of America. The money is now deposited at the office of the HERALD AND UNION.

Nov. 6th, 1876. **GEORGE MARLETTE.**

A poster in the collection of the Hayes Memorial Library of Fremont, Ohio.

Torchlight parades during the tense campaign of 1876 evoked partisan pride.

Many Democratic "floaters" who voted several times on election day were arrested.

Before the Election: Cartoonist Nast was quite confident the Republican Party would easily trample Samuel Tilden and Thomas Hendricks, the Democratic nominees for President and Vice President.

After the Election: Nast's elephant, battered and bandaged, moans with Pyrrhus, "Another such victory and I am undone." Hayes was elected by a margin of a single electoral vote.

HURRAH FOR THE HAYES TICKET, ALL.

Words by T. K. PREUSS.

GOOD-BYE.

Chorus.

COME, Freemen, assemble, and answer the call,
　That swells up from mountain and dale,
The shout has gone forth, we must conquer or fall,
　And our enemy fiercely assail.

Chorus.—Then hurrah for the Hayes Ticket, all,
　　As thousands respond to the call,
　　For our cause it is just,
　　And win it we must,
　　With the Hayes Ticket, Wheeler, and all.

2 Shall we supinely rest in this beautiful land,
　Where peace and all harmony dwell,
And see the despoiler, with bold, ruthless hand,
　Break the Union we love but too well?—Cho.

3 All tyrants shall tremble where'er our flag waves,
　In lands where base fetters are worn,

Where despots are worshipped by grovelling slaves,
　And freedom is yet to be born.—Cho.

4 Hayes, Wheeler, those champions and heroes so bold,
　With their statesman-like record so square,
Shall rally the people in numbers untold,
　Till their shouts fairly ring thro' the air.—Cho.

5 Shall it ever be said, when our shackles are made,
　And our rights under foot have been trod;
The Union has perished, her progress delayed,
　For no freeman can live on her sod?—Cho.

6 Up! up! all Republicans, eagerly fight,
　Your sons are no grovelling slaves,
Our banner now floats in a halo of light,
　And must win now wherever it waves.—Cho.

"Brave Rutherford Hayes" and "We Will Not Vote For Tilden" were other campaign songs.

Senator Roscoe Conkling, rival of Hayes and Blaine for the nomination of 1876.

Rep. William A. Wheeler, Hayes' running mate, helped found the G.O.P. in N.Y.

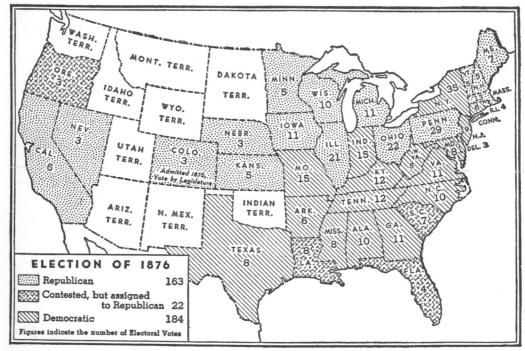

ELECTION OF 1876

▒	Republican	163
▩	Contested, but assigned to Republican	22
⫽	Democratic	184

Figures indicate the number of Electoral Votes

Hayes' defeat seemed certain on November 8, 1876, the day after the elections were held. Tilden, the Democratic candidate, appeared to have 4,300,590 popular and 196 electoral votes. Hayes, on the other hand, had but 4,036,298 popular and 173 electoral votes. However, serious doubt arose as to the validity of voting practices in Oregon and several southern states. Investigation by a special commission created by Congress revealed many conflicts and irregularities. Subsequently, Hayes was assigned 185 electoral votes; 184 went to Tilden.

Settling the disputed election of 1876 was the difficult task of a special electoral commission.

Violence threatened until resistance to the decision in favor of Hayes was discouraged by Democratic chieftains. Talk of "Tilden or Blood" had ominous overtones. Many threats were made against Hayes' life and an attempt to assassinate him was almost successful.

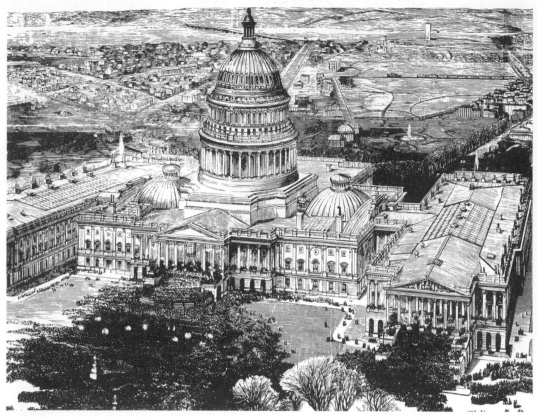

A sketch of Capitol Hill on inauguration day; note sparsely populated city in the background.

A torchlight procession, fireworks, and gay festivities heralded the inauguration.

"He serves his party best who serves his country best," Hayes declared in his unpretentious inaugural address on March 5, 1877. Since March 4th fell on a Sunday and since Grant's term officially ended at noon on that day, the new President was originally sworn into office in a private ceremony at midnight on March 3rd. Chief Justice Morrison R. Waite administered the oath on both occasions. The above photograph was taken by Mathew Brady.

A vivid pen and ink drawing of the White House during its occupancy by Hayes.

Patronage seekers were usually disappointed.

PRESIDENT HAYES AND CABINET.
1877.

Left to right, top to bottom: George W. McCrary, Secretary of War; Charles Devens, Attorney General; William M. Evarts, Secretary of State; President Hayes; John Sherman, Secretary of the Treasury; Carl Schurz, Secretary of the Interior; David M. Key, Postmaster General; Richard W. Thompson, Secretary of the Navy.   In the opinion of historian Harry J. Carman, Hayes appointed an "able cabinet" and "courageously supported officials who were applying reform methods in their departments."   Secretary of the Interior Schurz, an outspoken critic of Grant's policies, initiated the protection of forests on public domains, liberalized assistance to Indians, and introduced competitive examinations for posts in his department.

"An era of peace and good fellowship" and disbandonment of illegal organizations were results of Hayes' conciliatory policies, Harpers Weekly reported to its readers.

Northern "reconstruction" of the South ended on April 10, 1877 when Hayes withdrew the last federal troops from South Carolina.

In restoring the South to its original status in the Union without any restraints, Hayes alarmed "Old Democratic Party", the lady at the left, who is moaning "My child! My child! Oh dear! He's stolen my child!" But Columbia gratefully declares, "Oh bless you, sir." Despite its indebtedness to Hayes, the South remained solidly Democratic.

Miss America seems to find the company of Rutherford Hayes preferable to that of crochety Tilden.

President Hayes' appointment of famed poet James Russell Lowell as Minister to Spain in 1877 inspired this delightful caricature by Thomas Nast.

Secretary of Interior Carl Schurz frequently entertained the Hayes family.

"A Pow-Wow at the White House" shows President Hayes with tribal chieftains. To his left is Secretary of Interior Carl Schurz, the President's daughter, and Mrs. Hayes. "Many, if not most, of our Indian wars," Hayes frankly informed Congress, "have had their origin in broken promises and acts of injustice on our part." Supported by the President, Interior Secretary Carl Schurz instituted far-reaching reforms in the treatment of Indians by his department.

Although Hayes encountered opposition to his appointment of Cabinet members unsympathetic to patronage customs, Congress empowered him to institute civil service reforms.

"The stalwart members of his own (Hayes') party, as well as those partisans who were avid for office and power," William Starr Myers relates, "were aroused to bitter opposition by his attempts to introduce civil service reform and the merit system in appointments . . . But courageously and without a moment's hesitation he went ahead and did what he thought was right, and what succeeding years have proved was right . . . He paved the way for much of the reform and administrative and financial progress of the next two decades."

Sentinel Hayes to spoilsmen: "You can't come in here, gentlemen."

"Why Take a Crooked Road When There Is a Straight One?"—a contemporary cartoon endorsing the resumption of specie payments.

Despite dire predictions of a run on the nation's gold reserve, confidence in the government was such that, as the above telegram reports, only $40,000 in greenbacks were presented for exchange when **specie payment** was resumed.   President Hayes was pleased.

Free land and free speech attracted ever increasing numbers of immigrants from foreign lands.

This New Orleans levee scene reflects the prosperity enjoyed by the nation toward the end of Hayes' administration. A failure of overseas crops turned the balance of trade to America's favor.

President Hayes receiving the first Chinese Minister to the United States on Sept. 28, 1878.

Scientific explorations of the uncharted resources of the west led to the establishment of the United States Geological Survey as a permanent bureau of the Department of the Interior in 1879.

"The Cinderella of the Republican Party and Her Haughty Sisters", a Puck caricature. As the ele[ctions] of 1880 drew near, ex-President Grant (center) was favored for another term by the pow[er]ful Senator Roscoe Conkling (right); President Hayes (left) was by-passed quite conspicuous[ly]

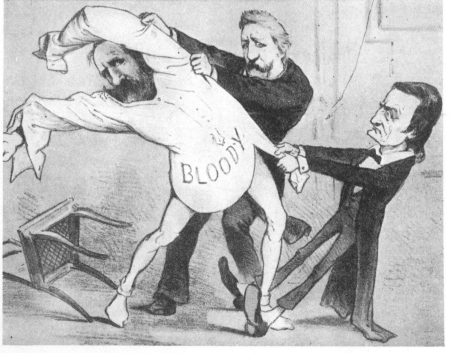

In some circles Hayes was unpopular because he objected to waving "the bloody shirt" at the South despite urgings of James G. Blaine and William Evarts.

"The administr[a]tion of Preside[nt] Hayes," declar[ed] historian Benjam[in] B. Kendrick, "[is] notable principal[ly] for the pacifi[fi]cation polic[y] adopted with r[e]spect to th[e] Southern state[s] bringing abou[t] the end of th[e] 'carpet-bag go[v]ernments' . . . Th[is] action brough[t] Hayes into shar[p] conflict with man[y] of the politic[al] leaders of h[is] party. It, how[-]ever, made mo[re] rapid the slow r[e]covery of th[e] South from th[e] effects of the wa[r] and was benefici[ci]al to the nation[.]

Uncle Sam in the 1870's: "The World Is My Market; My Customers Are All Mankind." An inevitable result of rapid agricultural and industrial development after the Civil War, foreign trade was playing a vital role in the life of the nation. Increasingly the world was looking to the United States as one of the chief sources of supply for food as well as manufactured articles. In the decade ending in 1880, American business with China alone amounted to nearly eighty million dollars, a sum greater than the total debt of the Revolutionary War which timid souls thought the young republic would never pay. The opening of vast new natural resources, abundance of farm products, expansion and diversification of industry, and growth of commercial know-how placed the United States in a distinctly favored position internally and externally during Hayes' administration.

Union enrollments rose and labor conditions improved measurably as the 1880's approached.

Although he lacked the popularity of Grant and the abilities of Blaine, conscientious James Abram Garfield became the party's standard bearer on the thirty-sixth ballot of the 1880 convention when the Grant-Blaine deadlock made a dark horse compromise inevitable. However, his humble origin and record of public service stood him in good stead. Born of staunch New England stock in a log cabin near Orange, Ohio, he faced and surmounted hardship from his childhood. He was left fatherless when he was two years old and had to help his mother with farm chores just as soon as he was capable of making himself useful. Nevertheless he acquired sufficient education to graduate from Williams College with honors and to become a school teacher. After several years as president of Hiram Eclectic Institute, he was admitted to the Ohio bar and entered politics. At the outbreak of the Civil War he joined Union forces as a Lieutenant Colonel and served with such distinction that Lincoln promoted him to the rank of Major General. Elected to Congress in 1864, he represented Ohio in that body for seventeen years.

Guiding horses along the Ohio Canal tow-path was a boyhood occupation Garfield enjoyed.

Garfield's home in Mentor, Ohio, where he resided prior to his election as President

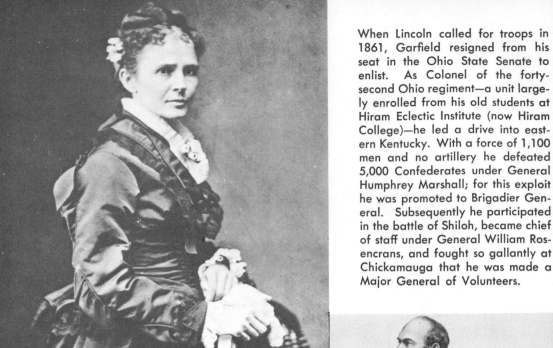

When Lincoln called for troops in 1861, Garfield resigned from his seat in the Ohio State Senate to enlist. As Colonel of the forty-second Ohio regiment—a unit largely enrolled from his old students at Hiram Eclectic Institute (now Hiram College)—he led a drive into eastern Kentucky. With a force of 1,100 men and no artillery he defeated 5,000 Confederates under General Humphrey Marshall; for this exploit he was promoted to Brigadier General. Subsequently he participated in the battle of Shiloh, became chief of staff under General William Rosencrans, and fought so gallantly at Chickamauga that he was made a Major General of Volunteers.

Mrs. James A. Garfield, the former Lucretia Rudolph.

A photograph of Garfield reading to his daughter Molly in 1867, the year in which he became Chairman of the House Committee on Military Affairs. "During Garfield's service in the House," according to Senator Samuel Hoar, "he was the leader of its best thought. Everything he did and said manifested the serious, reverent love of excellence. He was ever grave, earnest, addressing himself only to the reason and conscience of his auditors. You will search his speeches in vain for an appeal to a base motive or an evil passion. He was remarkably independent in forming his judgments and inflexible in adhering to them on all great essential occasions."

Garfield with his family in an 1880 lithograph. Leaning toward him is Mrs. Garfield; the elderly lady is his mother. Daughter Molly is at the piano; standing next to her is James, the eldest son. The youngsters are sons Harry, Abram, and Irving. James served as Secretary of Interior in the Cabinet of Theodore Roosevelt; Harry became the head of Williams College. "President Garfield was a man of indefatigable industry and vast information," declared an eminent contemporary. "He seemed constantly possessed by an intelligent curiosity in regard to all subjects. He had a tenacious memory. Its stores were always ready at hand for use on all occasions. There has been no man in public life in my time, except Charles Sumner, who was always so glad to render any service in his power to literature and science."

The Republican convention held in Chicago in June 1880 selected Garfield as a compromise candidate on the thirty-sixth ballot when a deadlock developed between nominees Grant and Blaine. Earlier in the same year Garfield had been chosen to represent Ohio in the U.S. Senate, but he became Chief Executive before he could take his seat in that chamber. Contrary to precedent, he took an unusually active part in the campaign for his election, making more than seventy speeches; until then it was customary for a candidate to let his supporters do most of the campaigning.

"That Republican Animal Will Carry It". Confident that Garfield and his running mate Chester Arthur would win the election of 1880, Thomas Nast drew this cartoon for Harper's Weekly.

175

TRUTH,

THE WHOLE TRUTH, AND NOTHING BUT THE TRUTH.

NO. 313.   NEW YORK, SATURDAY, OCTOBER 23, 1880.   PRICE ONE CENT.

GARFIELD'S POLITICAL DEATH WARRANT.

HIS INFAMOUS LETTER ADVOCATING THE INCREASED IMMIGRATION OF CHINESE CHEAP LABOR.

FAC SIMILE OF THE LETTER IN WHICH HE DECLARES HIMSELF ADVERSE TO THE LABORING MAN'S INTEREST, AND IN FAVOR OF THE EMPLOYERS' UNION—ADVISING THE EMPLOYMENT OF THE CHEAPEST LABOR AVAILABLE.

Facsimile of the front page of "Truth", a short-lived Democratic newspaper containing one of the most blatant falsehoods in American political history—a forged letter in which Garfield purportedly expressed subservience to big business and advocated increased immigration of cheap Chinese labor. The letter achieved a sensation, causing considerable harm before it was proved a forgery. Its real author went to prison for eight years.

Chester A. Arthur was selected as Garfield's running mate with the support of Grant's backers.

Puck's cartoonist was confident that Garfield would succeed Hayes despite strong competition.

FARMER GARFIELD
Cutting a Swath to the White House.

In the same process Democratic rival General Winfield Scott Hancock was uprooted from the political scene. Garfield won by an electoral vote of 214 to 155 for Hancock.

"The Republican Pachyderm Alive and Kicking" expressed Thomas Nast's confidence in Garfield's victory. Contrary to precedent, Garfield personally campaigned intensively, delivering more than seventy addresses. This was a new departure in that previous candidates left most of the speech making up to supporters. Although he won the election handily in terms of electoral votes, the popular vote was quite close; his plurality was less than ten thousand votes. General Hancock was even stronger than most Democratic candidates in the traditionally solid South. Republican votes below the Mason-Dixon line fell off as much as fifty percent in some states. Elsewhere the contest was so close that Hancock carried California by 78 votes, Nevada by 81 votes, and New Jersey by 2010 votes. Garfield, on the other hand, did well in most Northern and Western states, but carried Oregon by only 671 votes, Colorado by 3,203, and Connecticut by 2,661. The total popular vote was 4,454,416 for Garfield and 4,444,952 for Hancock. In a private letter to Senator John Sherman, Garfield expressed the belief that "the distrust of the solid South, and of adverse financial legislation, have been the chief factors in the contest."

The President-elect en route to the Capitol for the inaugural ceremonies.

Garfield being sworn into office as the twentieth President of the United States.

A brilliant inaugural ball was held in Washington's impressive new National Museum.

Watching the inaugural parade from the Capitol's vantage point.

The new administration augured well for the unity and prosperity of the nation, it seemed to cartoonist Nast. In his first official pronouncement as President, Garfield discussed the racial question in the South in temperate but firm words, stating that "under our institutions there was no middle ground for the Negro race between slavery and equal citizenship. There can be no permanent disfranchised peasantry in the United States." Acknowledging the peril of an uneducated electorate, he added that "to the South this question is of supreme importance. But the responsibility for the existence of slavery did not rest upon the South alone."

Top: "Welcome to All', a cartoon Joseph Keppler drew for Puck in 1880, was considered a tribute to Republican achievements since Lincoln's election in 1860.

Bottom: "Power Behind the Throne" was Thomas Nast's interpretation of the keen rivalry between Roscoe Conkling and James Blaine for White House influence.

Garfield's cabinet (left to right, top to bottom): Thomas J. Kirkwood, Secretary of the Interior; Thomas L. James, Postmaster General; William Windom, Secretary of the Treasury; Wayne MacVeagh, Attorney General; President Garfield; James G. Blaine, Secretary of State; Robert T. Lincoln, Secretary of War; William H. Hunt, Secretary of the Navy.

Senator Roscoe Conkling quarreling with President Garfield over patronage appointments.

Blaine amused the nation with his derisive reference to Conkling's "turkey gobbler strut".

"The Spoil-ed" Thomas Nast entitled this cartoon. Senators Conkling and Thomas Platt are kicking over the traces because Garfield turned down their nominees for government posts.

Conkling and Platt lost their heads, it seemed to Nast, when they took the drastic step of resigning from the Senate in protest against Garfield policies with which they disagreed.

186

The assassination of Garfield by a disappointed office seeker as the 1881, scarcely four months after his inauguration, awakened the Chief Executive entered a Washington railway station on July 2, nation to the urgent need for competitive civil service requirements.

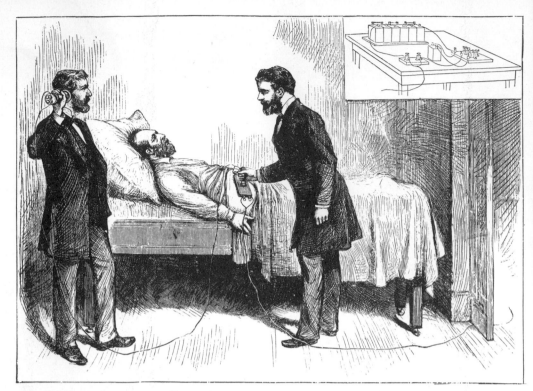

An electrical device specially made by inventor Alexander Graham Bell was used in an effort to detect the exact location of the assassin's bullet in the fast-sinking President.

Paying homage to the deceased President as his body lay in state in the Capitol rotunda. Garfield battled with death for ten weeks while the nation prayed for his recovery.

Elegant Chester Alan Arthur, as **Roger Butterfield** has so aptly said, "looked more like a President of the United States than any man since Washington." Tall, handsome, and courtly, he cut an impressive but somewhat lonely figure. Shadowed by the tragedy of Garfield's death that raised him to power and by the mistakes he had made as New York's Collector of Customs, he met his Presidential obligations with integrity and almost total disregard for old friends who expected him to resurrect the spoils system.

Arthur was born in this Fairfield, Vermont, shack on October 5, 1830. Of Scotch-Irish descent, he was the son of the Reverend William Arthur and Malvina (Stone) Arthur.

An expert angler, Arthur was considered "one of the country's best salmon fishers."

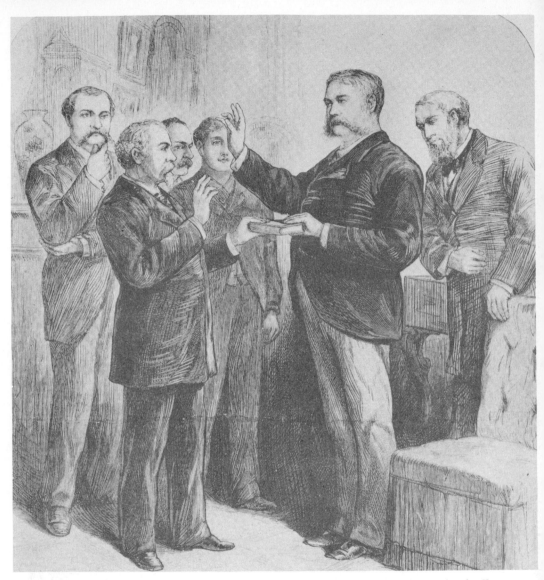

Arthur being sworn in as twenty-first President of the United States. The oath of office was administered in New York at half past one in the morning of September 20, 1881; Judge John R. Brady of the New York Supreme Court officiated. Among those on hand was Elihu Root, then a novice in politics. An opponent of slavery, Arthur first attracted attention when as a young lawyer he won the famous "Lemmon slave case" in which it was established that Negroes could shake off their shackles when they stepped on free soil. During the Civil War he served as Inspector General and Quartermaster General in New York. In 1871 Grant appointed him the Collector of Customs for the port of New York, but criticism of his conduct led to his removal by President Hayes in 1878. A leader of the "Stalwart" wing of the Republican Party, he was elected Garfield's Vice President chiefly with the support of that group. Apprehensions about his policies and abilities arose when he assumed the Presidency after Garfield's death, but, contrary to journalistic expectation, he fulfilled the responsibilities of the nation's highest office judiciously and conscientiously. If his administration lacked dramatic achievement, it was also devoid of friction and discord.

While vacationing in fashionable Newport, Rhode Island, President Arthur was a cynosure of both male and female eyes.

(Top) During his tenure as Vice President Arthur aroused the displeasure of cartoonist Thomas Nast because he had sought to effect a reconciliation with Senators Conkling and Platt after their bitter quarrels with President Garfield. To Nast, as well as to some of Garfield's close friends, it seemed that Arthur had gone out of his way to shine the shoes of the recalcitrant Senators

(Bottom) After assuming the Presidency, however, Arthur rejected the advances of Conkling and company. "Realizing to the full the obligations of his new position," historian Allan Nevins relates, "Arthur turned a cold shoulder to his old associates in politics, made appointments with careful regard to fitness and gave his Administration an admirable dignity and decorum. He signed some excellent legislation, showed courage in vetoing a bad rivers and harbors bill, and left office high in the regard of the nation"

The President's private dining room in the White House was the essence of dignity and decorum. An eye-catching feature of the vestibule was a colored glass screen specially made by Tiffany's.

During the 1880s feminine lobbyists, reportedly engaged by "the interests", made their debut on Capitol Hill. Democrats charged them with being "tools of the Republicans", but to all indications they operated on a strictly non-partisan basis, directing their charms on Republicans and Democrats alike. Their party lines were uniquely their own. "The 1880s," relates Karl Schriftgiesser in his history of lobbying, "saw a great increase in the activity of lobbyists in Washington and a refinement of their methods. were brought to bear upon its members not to succumb to the lure of tariff reduc- When the Democrats controlled Congress in 1884-1886 great and successful pressures tions . . . It was in this general period that minority interests began to organize."

The modernization of the Navy was vigorously pushed by Arthur. He showed keen personal interest when watching warship maneuvers during summer training operations.

Post Office Department services were expanded; letter rates were cut to two cents.

The first Labor Day parade in New York on September 5, 1882, reflected trade union growth.

The emergence of the labor movement was signified by the growth of the Knights of Labor from 10,000 members in 1879 to 700,000 in 1886. It was in the latter year that the American Federation of Labor was founded.

An increasing number of women were entering the labor market as white collar and industrial workers. These young ladies manned the first telephone switchboard installed in Richmond, Virginia.

The present Department of Labor is an outgrowth of the Bureau of Labor established under President Arthur's administration in 1884. It was housed in this Washington building opposite the Treasury.

Lawless cutting of fences characterized feuds between cattlemen and crop-raising homesteaders.

Settlers of sturdy stock played a leading role in the exciting drama of western expansion.

In Nebraska the enterprising Chrisman sisters obtained homesteads totaling some 740 acres.

Immigrants from northern Europe helped transform the rugged plains into fertile farmlands.

For the tired, the poor, and the huddled masses of the earth, the United States opened wider its gates in the 1880's. By the end of the decade five million more immigrants had fused their lives in the American melting pot. Charles F. Ulrich painted the above picture.

At county fairs the American way of life took on vivid shapes, colors, and sounds.

A large number of devices designed to make housework simpler made their appearance during the 1880's. Inventiveness was prolific.

Ingenious washing machines offered welcome relief from the humdrum routines of the past and piped-in gas permitted mother to catch up on her reading while dinner practically cooked itself.

Father could (and sometimes did) help with domestic chores by walking a monstrous cleaning contraption over the carpets.

Thomas Edison's experimental electric railway attracted both admiration and ridicule.

The horizons of American culture broadened perceptibly—and audibly—with the opening of the Metropolitan Opera House in New York City on October 22, 1883.

Edison was literally electrifying American life and industry via his **first power** station.

One of the most bitterly disappointed figures in American history, James Gillespie Blaine saw victory snatched from him again and again. When the convention of 1876 opened he had virtually enough votes to obtain the nomination on the very first ballot—yet he was defeated by a dark horse, Rutherford B. Hayes. Four years later his chances of receiving the nomination seemed excellent, but party unity was almost torn asunder by forces seeking a third term for Grant; again he was defeated by a dark horse, James A. Garfield. Finally, in 1884, he was chosen the party's standard bearer and his election appeared to be a certainty but an inept remark by an obscure supporter led to his defeat by only 1,149 votes. For the first time since 1860 a Democrat, Grover Cleveland, became the President of the United States.

The great-grandson of Col. Ephraim Blaine, Commissary General of the American Revolutionary Army, James G. Blaine was born in West Brownsville, Pennsylvania, in 1830. His father was a Presbyterian of Scotch-Irish blood; his mother was a devout Catholic. Educated at Washington College, he studied law while teaching at the Pennsylvania Institute for the Blind. In 1854 he moved to Maine, assumed the editorship of the Kennebec Journal, and became the state's most prominent Republican. He served in the front ranks of the party for almost forty years, achieving considerable distinction as Speaker of the House of Representatives from 1869 to 1875 and as a United States Senator during the period 1876-1881. Of his college days Irving Stone relates: "He was tall for his age, gawky, with a large nose . . . He did not drink, smoke, gamble, or swear; his only vice was politics; he took to politics the way other boys took to baseball, was so much a natural in the field that it was later said of him that he was born under the rotunda of the Capitol in Washington."

Blaine at nineteen.

Replying to Democratic charges that he had improperly assisted several business firms, **Blaine** presented his case to the House of Representatives in a melodramatic defense which convinced most of the legislators of his integrity, but the episode militated against his securing the nomination for President in 1876 and necessitated the selection of Rutherford B. Hayes.

Meeting in the same Chicago hall, delegates to the 1884 convention of the Republican Party chose Blaine on the fifth ballot with 541 votes. In endorsing Blaine, Judge West declared: "Nominate him and the campfires and beacon lights will illuminate the continent from the Golden Gate to Cleopatra's Needle." A deafening cheer arose.

A pandemonium of approval broke out when Blaine's name was put in nomination at the Chicago convention in 1880. His supporters defeated the attempt to nominate Grant for a third term but, after six days and thirty-five ballots, they realized they could not secure the nomination for Blaine; their votes were then switched to James A. Garfield.

While Chicagoans milled around the convention hall in 1884, the delegates inside drew up a platform which did not suit party elements opposed to Blaine.

Blaine's running mate, John A. Logan (below with his family), saw duty in the war with Mexico, became active in Illinois politics, entered the House of Representatives as a Democrat in 1858, succeeded General Sherman as Commander of the Fifteenth Army Corps during the Civil War, returned to Congress on the Republican ticket in 1866, and became a Senator in 1871. Memorial Day became a national holiday because of his efforts.

The platform on which they ran promised "quick and faithful response to the demands of the people for the freedom and equality of all men; for a united nation assuring the rights of all citizens; for the elevation of labor; for an honest currency; for purity in legislation . . ."

Contemporary artists made the most—as well as the worst—of Robert G. Ingersoll's reference to Blaine as "a plumed knight". Favorable and unfavorable versions of the above cartoon, originally drawn by Joseph Keppler, appeared during 1884 campaign.

THE · GREAT · NATIONAL · GAME

LAST · MATCH · OF · THE · SEASON · TO BE DECIDED · NOV · 11TH · 1884 ·

The general idea of this delightful cartoon is clear, but the exact meaning is somewhat obscure. Pitcher Blaine is about to throw a curved one to President Arthur (whom he struck out), while Democrat Tilden, the catcher, evidently keeps his eye on the ball for his own partisan purposes.

Agnostic lawyer-orator Robert G. Ingersoll supported Blaine eloquently—and disadvantageously. "Like an armed warrior, like a plumed knight", he fervently declared at the 1876 convention, "James G. Blaine marched down the halls of the American Congress and threw his shining lance full and fair against the brazen foreheads of the defamers of his country and the maligners of her honor. For the Republican Party to desert this gallant leader now is as though an army should desert their general upon the field of battle."

Other popular campaign songs were entitled "Wake, O Republicans, Wake", "Hold the Fort for Blaine and Logan," "Dinna Ye Hear the Slogan," and "Our Plumed Knight Leads the Way."

"Our Republican Leaders", a lithograph of 1884. 1. Blaine. 2. Logan. 3. George F. Edmunds. 4. Ulysses S. Grant. 5. Chester A. Arthur. 6. George F. Hoar. 7. W. E. Chandler. 8. Frederick T. Frelinghuysen. 9. John F. Miller. 10. Robert T. Lincoln. 11. J. Donald Cameron. 12. John Sherman. 13. George P. Robinson. 14. Benjamin Harrison. 15. John J. Ingalls. 16. Name uncertain. 17. Walter Q. Gresham. 18. William B. Allison. This lithograph was widely distributed.

Variations of "Another Voice for Cleveland" (left) were played up by Republican papers when the Buffalo Evening News made the sensational charge that Cleveland was the father of an illegitimate offspring of an illicit relationship with a widow named Maria Halpin. This inspired a popular ditty:

"Ma! Ma! Where's my pa?
"Gone to the White House,
"Ha! Ha! Ha!

To Democrats it seemed that Cleveland was being crucified in retaliation for attacks on Blaine's integrity. Although Cleveland admitted he had been intimate with Mrs. Halpin, he emphatically insisted he was not the father of her child.

Dissatisfied with Blaine's nomination, Carl Schurz (center) bolted from the party along with Henry Ward Beecher, Charles W. Eliot, and others.

He is always in the way—
        Blaine of Maine ;
And in session every day
        Raises Cain ;
When his prodding makes us roar,
Then he lacerates the sore,
Till we holler more and more—
        Blaine of Maine.
How he boxes us around—
        Blaine of Maine ;
Now and then we're on the ground,
        Half insane ;
Frequently to grass we go ;
This is temporary though,
For we rally from the blow,
And prepare to eat our crow,
But he stands us in a row,
And he smites us high and low,
Till we shiver in our woe,
And he keeps us whirling so,
That we have the vertigo—

Doggerel of Democratic Congressmen.

A formidable revolt by Republicans opposed to Blaine—his supporters nicknamed them "Mugwumps"—disrupted party unity.

The popular vote was painfully close. Blaine's loss of New York's strategic electoral vote by less than 1500 popular votes gave Grover Cleveland a hairline victory.

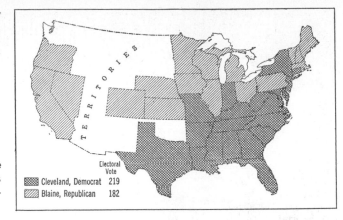

Electoral Vote

▨ Cleveland, Democrat   219
▧ Blaine, Republican   182

The votes in the north and middle west were so close that recounts kept the final results somewhat uncertain for almost a week.

Almost on the eve of the election, Blaine was dealt a crushing blow by a seemingly inconsequential incident. In the course of a routine reception for a group of New York clergymen, a Dr. Burchard made a speech in which he ineptly remarked: "We are Republicans and don't propose to leave our party and identify ourselves with the party whose antecedents have been rum, Romanism, and rebellion". Blaine took no notice of the anti-Catholic slur, possibly because he did not happen to hear it. However, Democratic newspapers took considerable note of it, giving the impression that he was personally responsible for what was said. Despite the consequent loss of New York's large Catholic voting population, Blaine came within a scant 1500 votes of winning the state's decisive electoral backing. He unquestionably would have been elected President if it had not been for Burchard's tactless remark.

INTER-AMERICAN
CONFERENCES

UNITED STATES

Washington
1889, 1928

MEXICO

Havana
1928, 1940

CUBA

Mexico City
1901

CENTRAL
AMERICA

Panama
1826, 1939

VENEZUELA

COLOMBIA

BR. DU. FR.
GUIANA

ECUADOR

PERU

Lima
1938

BRAZIL

BOLIVIA

PARAGUAY

Rio de Janeiro
1906

CHILE

ARGENTINA

Santiago
1923

Buenos Aires
1910, 1936

URU-
GUAY

Montevideo
1933

GOOD NEIGHBOR POLICY

An early architect of the Good Neighbor Policy, Blaine laid the foundations for inter-American cooperation during his brief term as Garfield's Secretary of State. In 1889, while serving as Harrison's Secretary of State, he called the first Pan American Conference, which paved the way to the establishment of the Pan American Union with headquarters in Washington, D. C.

If short, cautious Benjamin Harrison seldom exuded warmth, he at least made up for this failing in substantial degree with his distinguished lineage. Great grandson of Benjamin Harrison, signer of the Declaration of Independence, and grandson of William Henry Harrison, ninth President of the United States, he worked on his father's Ohio farm in his youth, graduated from Miami University, and was earning his living as an attorney in Indianapolis when he answered Lincoln's call for enlistments in 1861. Although he preferred to continue his law practice, Indiana's legislature elected him to the United States Senate in 1881. However, he failed of reelection in 1887 and was all but forgotten when fate—and party differences at the convention of 1888 — made possible his selection as a dark horse candidate for the Presidency. The prospect of election evidently left him somewhat unenthusiastic. His acceptance of the Presidency, he reportedly confided to a friend, "would be attended with more diffidence and reluctance than I have ever experienced before in my life." Fellow Republican Senator George F. Hoar once made the following estimate of Harrison: "He lacked what gave Mr. Blaine so great a charm, the quality of an agreeable and gracious manner. He had little tact in dealing with individuals . . . Blaine would refuse a request in a way that would seem like doing a favor. Harrison would grant a request in a way which seemed as if he were denying it. An eminent western Senator said to me once what, of course, was a great exaggeration, that if Harrison were to address an audience of 10,000 men, he would capture them all. But if each one of them were presented to him in private, he would make them his enemy."

During the Civil War, Harrison rose from the rank of Lieutenant
to that of Brigadier General. He fought in several major battles.

Born on Aug. 20, 1833, at North Bend, Ohio, Harrison received his early education in a log
schoolhouse near family farm. At 21 he moved to Indianapolis, practiced law, entered politics.

President Harrison's family (left to right): Mrs. Harrison, grandson Benjamin H. McKee, daughter Mrs. J. R. McKee, granddaughter Mary L. McKee, and the Rev. Dr. Scott, Mrs. Harrison's father. This photograph by Charles Parker was evidently taken in the White House in 1889.

The first Mrs. Benjamin Harrsion (nee Caroline Lavinia Scott) became the head of the Daughters of the American Revolution when that organization was founded in 1890. She bore her husband a son and a daughter. In 1896, four years after her death, her niece, Mrs. Mary Scott Lord Dimmock, became the second Mrs. Harrison.

"Harrison's distinguishing trait of character," in the opinion of historian-diplomat John Watson Foster, "to which his success is to be most largely attrib uted, was his thoroughness. He was somewhat reserved in manner, and this led to the charge in political circles that he was cold and unsympathetic; but no one gathered around him more devoted and loyal friends, and his dignified bearing in and out of office commanded the hearty respect of his countrymen." The picture below was taken by George Prince in the winter of 1888.

Close runner-up for the Presidential nomination in 1888 was Chauncey Depew, shown above with his wife in 1922. He remained a prominent Republican until his death in 1928.

Levi P. Morton, Harrison's Vice President, was previously a banker, Congressman, and Minister to France. In 1895 he was elected the Governor of New York State.

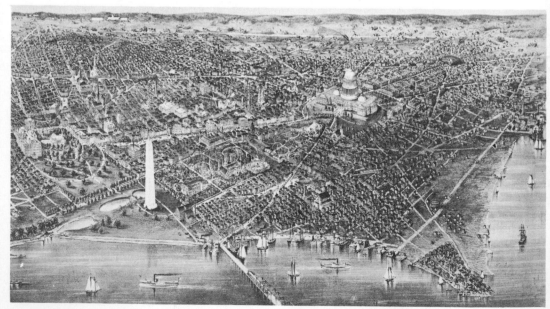

What the nation's capital looked like to a Currier and Ives lithograph artist of the 1890's.

The tariff question was a dominant—and highly controversial—issue in 1888.

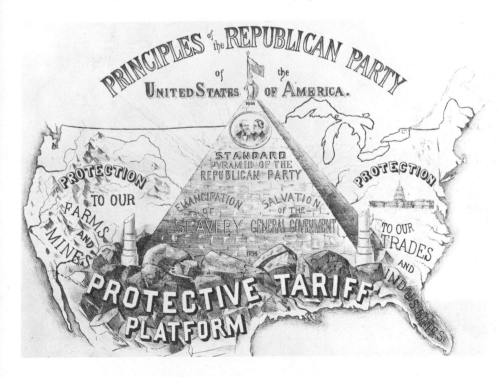

They won the election of 1888 with a majority of electoral votes, defeating Democrat Grover Cleveland and his running mate Allen G. Thurman. Harrison secured the Republican nomination when backers of Senators John Sherman and Chauncey Depew failed to rally enough support

Scene at the Chicago convention at which Harrison was chosen as the standard bearer of the G.O.P. He was selected on the eighth ballot.

Rain fell in torrents when on March 4, 1889, Benjamin Harrison was sworn into office as twenty-third President of the United States   In spite of the distinctly inclement weather some 30,000 persons took part in the colorful inaugural parade while the President looked on in high spirits.

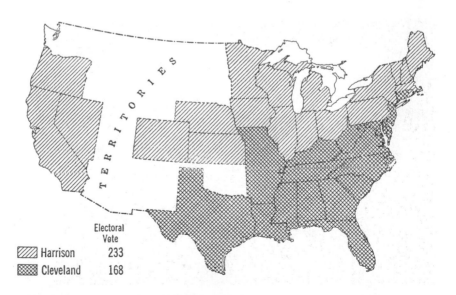

	Electoral Vote
Harrison	233
Cleveland	168

Although Harrison received 233 electoral votes, his popular vote (5,439,-853) was slightly smaller than that which went to Cleveland (5,540,329).

Reports from the Treasury forecast an economic upswing.

In celebrating the centennial anniversary of Washington's inauguration, Harrison personally participated in a dramatic reenactment of the first President's arrival in New York City.

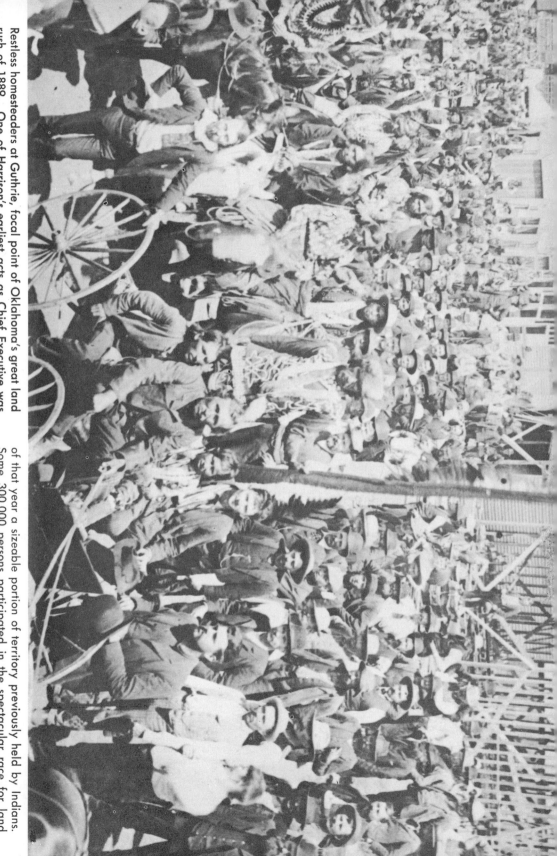

Restless homesteaders at Guthrie, focal point of Oklahoma's great land rush of 1889. One of Harrison's earliest acts as Chief Executive was of that year a sizeable portion of territory previously held by Indians. Some 300,000 persons participated in the spectacular race for land

Elected to Congress on the Republican ticket in 1885, Robert M. La Follette of Wisconsin (seen above with his wife and daughter Fola in 1924) worked closely with William McKinley in drafting the Tariff Act of 1890, which contained reciprocity features and lowered some duties.

The tariff policy of the Republican Party was considered the goose that laid the golden egg of prosperity for the American worker—much to the disappointment of Democrat Roger Q. Mill shown here urging the knifing of "protection" by "free trade".

Senator John Sherman

The monopoly problem as
conceived by Thomas Nast.

The most important legislation enacted during Harrison's administration was the Sherman Anti-Trust Act of 1890. Designed to protect commerce and the consumer against unlawful economic restraints and illegal monopolies, it struck a body blow to the powerful trusts. The man after whom this law was named, Senator John Sherman, was a leading member of the Republican Party from its inception. He helped found the party in Ohio, served as chairman of the powerful House Ways and Means and Senate Finance Committees, became Secretary of the Treasury under Hayes, and returned to the Senate in 1881. In 1880 and again in 1888 he came close to receiving the party's nomination for the Presidency. He retired from public life after a brief term as Secretary of State under McKinley.

President Harrison and his Cabinet in 1892 (left to right): Stephen B. Elkins, Secretary of War; John W. Noble, Secretary of the Interior; John W. Foster, Secretary of State; John Wanamaker, Postmaster General; President Harrison; Benjamin F. Tracey, Secretary of the Navy; Charles Foster, Secretary of the Treasury; Jeremiah M. Rusk, Secretary of Agriculture; and William Henry Harrison Miller, Attorney General. The last mentioned was evidently named after the President's grandfather. Blaine was Foster's predecessor as Secretary of State.

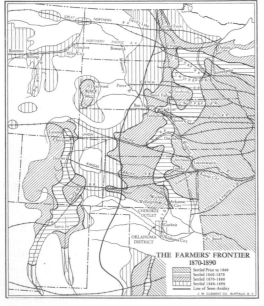

THE FARMERS' FRONTIER
1870-1890

Settled Prior to 1860
Settled 1860-1870
Settled 1870-1880
Settled 1880-1890
Line of Semi-Aridity

J. W. CLEMENT CO. BUFFALO, N. Y.

Some Democratic newspapers sharply criticized Harrison's appointment of John Wanamaker as Postmaster General on the ground that the latter was being repaid for his generous contributions to the Republican Party. "This gratuitous insult to the character and intentions of two perfectly honest, upright, and high-minded Americans," according to William Starr Myers, "fell of its own weight, and was merely another instance of that most unfortunate characteristic of reformers and other idealists which has its expression in a sinister lack of confidence in any one but themselves."

Encouraged by homestead legislation and continued federal aid for railroad construction, farmers surged out into the fertile western plains. Thirty bushels of wheat per acre or seventy of corn were not unusual in this area.

Among the leading members of Congress **during** Harrison's administration were Senator Matthew Quay (left in costume) and Rep. Thomas B. Reed (right), Speaker of the House.

Appointed a member of the Civil Service Commission by President Harrison, Theodore Roosevelt undertook to revitalize the merit system when he was but thirty years of age. During his association with the Commission more than 20,000 positions were put under the merit system.

During the bitter and sometimes violent struggle between midwestern Republicans and Populists in the 1890's, Kansas Governor Lewelling found it necessary to call out the militia when Populist advocates seized the state legislative chamber and proceeded to form their own government.

Order was maintained in the Topeka capitol by armed, specially appointed sergeants-at-arms.

Hardy Nebraska settlers of the 1890's posing in front of the sod dugout they called home. The first settlers found a prairie almost entirely without trees except along the streams and on rough uplands. To their forethought are due the pleasant groves and tree-lined roads seen today.

Protection of westerners from unfriendly Indians was still a major responsibility of Army personnel.

On June 7, 1892, Harrison was again nominated—this time on the first ballot at the convention held in Minneapolis. Confident of his reelection, Leslie's Illustrated News ran the above cartoon. Whitelaw Reid was chosen the Vice Presidential candidate.

Seats were quite scarce at the Minneapolis convention

Whitelaw Reid, N.Y. Tribune editor.

This extraordinary photo was taken on September 16, 1893, when Oklahoma's Cherokee Strip was opened to homesteaders.

They supervised opening of Oklahoma's Cherokee Strip for homestead settlement in 1893.

Stationed at Perry, the above agents of the General Land Office carried out the last official measure of Harrison's administration—an act authorizing homesteads in the Cherokee Strip and other Indian land.

Overnight, Perry became a forest of tents as thousands flocked in for Cherokee Strip land.

These homestead applicants mobbed the General Land Office quarters on Sept. 22, 1893.

As its population increased in the 1890's, Oklahoma Territory entered an era of rapid growth. Towns sometimes sprang up between breakfast and supper. Individual land allotments were made to Indians who previously lived on reservations.

This photo was taken at Orlando about an hour before the Cherokee Strip was opened.

Making steel by the Bessemer converter process was rapidly revolutionizing American industry.

Contemporary advertisements such as these reflect steadily rising standards of living.

241

Telegraphy, electricity, and the telephone were also changing American life—and appearance—in unexpected ways. New York City was practically enmeshed by overhanging wires in 1893.

242

Like most American Presidents, William McKinley was the son of humble, hardworking people. He was born of Scotch-Irish parentage on January 29, 1843, in Niles, Ohio. Illness interrupted his schooling, forcing him to suspend his studies at Allegheny College. He was a post office clerk when, at 18, he enlisted in the Union Army. By a curious twist of history, he was mustered into service by General John C. Fremont, first Republican candidate for President, and saw duty under Brigadier General Rutherford B. Hayes, who became the standard bearer of the party in 1876. Although inconspicuous, he gave a good account of himself in a score of Civil War battles and rose from private to Major (a title he cherished almost as much as that of President of the United States). Upon emerging from the conflict a fire-tried veteran of 22, he turned to the study of law, hung out his shingle in Canton, and entered the hurly-burly of politics. In 1876 he was elected to the House of Representatives, where he remained almost continuously until 1890. While Chairman of the House Ways and Means Committee he attained national prominence as the Republican Party's most forceful champion of the protective tariff system. Prior to his election as President in 1896, he served two terms as Governor of Ohio.

A photograph of McKinley (center) with Marcus A. Hanna (right) during a visit to Thomasville, Ohio. Mrs. McKinley is seated on the right.

Mrs. William McKinley in the 1890's.

McKinley's birthplace in Niles, Ohio.

1863 1859 1866

1864 1861

Sketches of McKinley prior to his election to Congress in 1876.

1871

At the Battle of Cornifax Ferry in September 1861, he participated in his first military engagement.

A lithograph of the President with his wife and mother. At the time of his marriage to Ida Saxton, daughter of an Ohio merchant, McKinley was the prosecuting attorney for Stark County. Two daughters were born in the Canton home depicted in the upper right hand corner. Such was McKinley's devotion to his wife, an invalid in her last years, that a Senator once remarked that the President made it hard for all other husbands in Washington because they were expected to live up to the example he set. His attachment to his mother, a devout Methodist, was also great. When he received news of his election as President, McKinley knelt down in prayer with his wife and mother. "Oh God, keep him humble," the old woman murmured as she pressed his hand.

Joseph B. Foraker's eloquent presentation of McKinley's candidacy helped clinch the nomination on the very first ballot of the Republican national convention held in St. Louis in the summer of 1896.

Delegates to the convention were strongly influenced in McKinley's favor by astute Marcus Alonzo Hanna, who lined up powerful support earlier in the year among Republicans throughout the country.

Maintenance of the gold standard and of the protective tariff system were the major planks of their platform. In opposing the "free and unrestricted coinage of silver" urged by William Jennings Bryan, 36-year-old Democratic nominee for President in 1896, McKinley held that his rival's proposal would undermine the economy. Campaign literature billed McKinley and Hobart as "the advance agents of prosperity"

THE REAL ISSUE

UNITED STATES MINT.

I do not know what you think about it, but I believe it is a good deal better to open up the mills of the United States to the labor of America than to open up the mints of the United States to the silver of the World.

McKinley's stand in this poster appealed to labor.

As in previous years, the trade unions favored the party's protective tariff policy because it bolstered wages and discouraged competition from cheap foreign labor. Friendship between McKinley and the unions dated back to 1876, when he took up the case of 34 striking coal miners charged with rioting. Although no other lawyer would take the case and he was warned by his friends against doing so, McKinley defended the miners and obtained the acquittal of all but one of them.

Arrayed against Bryan's "motley crew", McKinley's forces included disaffected Democrats.

Organized labor joined with business in opposing Bryan. His position on silver was considered tantamount to "repudiation" of Treasury obligations. McKinley enjoyed the confidence of captains of industry as well as of trade union leaders. With Samuel Gompers, long-time President of the American Federation of Labor, he was on cordial terms. "He would frequently ask me to the White House," Gompers noted in his autobiography, "to see him and sometimes I would ask for the privilege. At no time was I disappointed."

"Labor and Business Eye Their Common Enemy"

McKinley's "front porch" campaign, managed by Hanna, was unprecedented but effective. 251

Joseph B. Foraker helped Hanna groom McKinley for the Presidency. A former Governor of Ohio, he was elected to the U.S. Senate in 1896 and became a spokesman for the new administration.

As Chairman of the Republican National Committee, astute Marcus Alonzo Hanna was highly instrumental in mobilizing powerful support behind his friend and fellow-Ohioan William McKinley.

New Yorkers watching a McKinley-Hobart campaign parade on fashionable Fifth Avenue.

Selection of Garret A. Hobart, a close personal friend, as his running mate greatly pleased McKinley. Although not widely known, Hobart was highly esteemed as Vice Chairman of the Republican National Committee and as President of New Jersey's Senate.

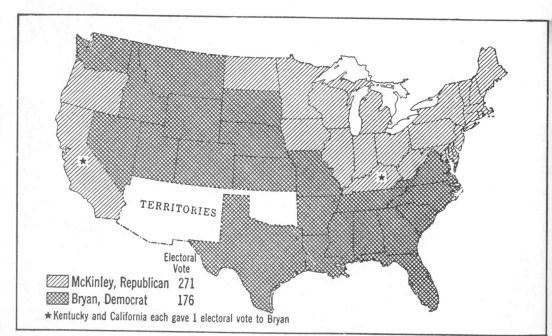

TERRITORIES

Electoral
Vote
McKinley, Republican 271
Bryan, Democrat 176
★ Kentucky and California each gave 1 electoral vote to Bryan

Democratic rival Bryan was overwhelmingly defeated by McKinley's vote of 7,098,474.

President-elect McKinley en route to his inauguration at the Capitol on March 4, 1897.

Grover Cleveland, the outgoing Chief Executive, looked on as McKinley was sworn in as the 25th President of the U.S. Chief Justice Melville W. Fuller administered the oath of office.

A photo of McKinley's wife and mother (front row right) watching his inauguration.

White House furnishings during McKinley's occupancy mirrored contemporary American tastes in interior decoration.

Distinguished visitors were entertained in the Red Room.

President McKinley and his Cabinet in 1897 (left to right around the table): McKinley; Lyman J. Gage, Secretary of the Treasury; John W. Griggs, Attorney General; John D. Long, Secretary of the Navy; James Wilson, Secretary of Agriculture; Cornelius N. Bliss, Secretary of the Interior; Charles E. Smith, Postmaster General; Russell A. Alger, Secretary of War; William R. Day, Secretary of State. Day later served as an Associate Justice of the Supreme Court.

Thousands paid homage to the memory of President Ulysses Grant when his body was interred in New York's impressive Riverside Drive tomb several weeks after McKinley's inauguration.

As Assistant Secretary of the Navy, Theodore Roosevelt was both brash and farsighted in ordering Commodore George Dewey to attack Spanish warships off the Philippine Islands upon the outbreak of expected hostilities, thus making sure that the first battle of the Spanish-American conflict would be fought far from U.S. waters. Only eight Americans were wounded in this battle.

Blowing up of the U.S. battleship Maine in Havana harbor on February 15, 1898, precipitated the short-lived but spectacular war with Spain. Some 260 men and officers aboard were killed.

NEW YORK JOURNAL
AND ADVERTISER.

FIRST EDITION.

NO. 5,572.   Copyright, 1898, by W. R. Hearst—NEW YORK, THURSDAY, FEBRUARY 17, 1898.—16 PAGES.   PRICE ONE CENT

The Journal will give $50,000 for information, furnished to it exclusively, that will convict the person who sank the Maine.

The Journal will give $50,000 for information, furnished to it exclusively, that will convict the person or persons who sank the Maine.

DESTRUCTION OF THE WAR SHIP MAINE WAS THE WORK OF AN ENEMY

$50,000!

$50,000 REWARD!
For the Detection of the Perpetrator of the Maine Outrage!

The New York Journal hereby offers a reward of $50,000 CASH which is FURNISHED TO IT EXCLUSIVELY, which will lead to the detection and conviction of the person, persons or government criminally responsible for the destruction of the Maine and the loss of 258 lives of the United States war ship Maine and the loss of 258 lives of American sailors.

No one is barred for the double, but misguided, etc. will only a few miserable dollars to bring as a spy or the arm to of a general enthusiast not thinking by any desires means, to revenge-tan and terrible or cripple tantamounting conspire.

This offer has been cabled to Europe and will be made public in every capital of the Continent and in London this morning.

The Journal believes that any man who can be bought to commit murder can also be bought to betray his comrades. FOR THE PERPETRATOR OF THIS OUTRAGE HAD ACCOMPLICES.
Life.   W. R. HEARST

Assistant Secretary Roosevelt Convinced the Explosion of the War Ship Was Not an Accident.

The Journal Offers $50,000 Reward for the Conviction of the Criminals Who Sent 258 American Sailors to Their Death. Naval Officers Unanimous That the Ship Was Destroyed on Purpose.

$50,000!

$50,000 REWARD!
For the Detection of the Perpetrator of the Maine Outrage!

The New York Journal hereby offers a reward of $50,000 CASH for information FURNISHED TO IT EXCLUSIVELY, which shall lead to the detection and conviction of the person, persons or government criminally responsible for the explosion which resulted in the destruction, at Havana, of the United States war ship Maine and the loss of 258 lives of American sailors.

The $50,000 CASH offered for the above information is on deposit with Wells, Fargo & Co. and will be paid upon the production of the conclusive evidence.

No one is barred, be he the double, but misguided, etc. will only a few miserable dollars to bring as a spy or the arm to of a general enthusiast not thinking by any desires means, to revenge-tan and terrible or cripple tantamounting conspire.

This offer has been cabled to Europe and will be made public in every capital of the Continent and in London this morning.

The Journal believes that any man who can be bought to betray his comrades. FOR THE PERPETRATOR OF THIS OUTRAGE HAD ACCOMPLICES.
Life.   W. R. HEARST

POWDER MAGAZINE

NAVAL OFFICERS THINK THE MAINE WAS DESTROYED BY A SPANISH MINE.

George Eugene Bryson, the Journal's special correspondent at Havana, cables that it is the secret opinion of many Spaniards in the Cuban capital, that the Maine was destroyed and 258 of her men killed by means of a submarine mine, or fixed torpedo. This is the opinion of several American naval authorities. The Spaniards, it is believed, arranged to have the Maine anchored over one of the harbor mines. Wires connected the mine with a powder magazine, and it is thought the explosion was caused by sending an electric current through the wire. It this can be proven, the brutal nature of the Spaniards will be shown by the fact that they waited to spring the mine until after all the men had returned for the night. The Maine's crew went to quarters where a number may have been lost.

Hidden Mine or a Sunken Torpedo Believed to Have Been the Weapon Used Against the American Man-of-War---Officers and Men Tell Thrilling Stories of Being Blown Into the Air Amid a Mass of Shattered Steel and Exploding Shells---Survivors Brought to Key West Scout the Idea of Accident---Spanish Officials Protest Too Much---Our Cabinet Orders a Searching Inquiry---Journal Sends Divers to Havana to Report Upon the Condition of the Wreck. Was the Vessel Anchored Over a Mine?

Assistant Secretary of the Navy Theodore Roosevelt says he is convinced that the destruction of the Maine in Havana Harbor was not an accident.

The Journal offers a reward of $50,000 for exclusive evidence that will convict the person, persons or Government criminally responsible for the destruction of the American battleship and the death of 258 of its crew.

The suspicion that the Maine was deliberately blown up grows stronger every hour. Not a single fact to the contrary has been produced.

Captain Sigsbee, of the Maine, and Consul-General Lee both urge that public opinion be suspended until they have completed their investigation. They are taking the course of tactful men who are convinced that there has been treachery.

Spanish Government officials are pressing forward all sorts of explanations of how it could have been an accident. The facts show that there was a report before the ship exploded, and that, had her magazine exploded, she would have sunk immediately.

Every naval expert in Washington says that if the Maine's magazine had exploded the whole vessel would have been blown to atoms.

The demand for war which followed in the wake of this news was overwhelming. Congress promptly voted fifty million dollars "as an emergency measure for national defense" and military enlistments rose sharply. Throughout the nation men and boys paraded with banners and buttons inscribed "Remember the Maine". For several months McKinley tried to avert war, but popular sentiment resulted in a declaration of hostilities against Spain on April 25, 1898.

Watching from a precarious position on the Olympia, Commodore George Dewey saw the guns under his command pound Spain's Asiatic fleet into scrap on May 1, 1898. He opened the decisive battle of Manila Bay with a terse order to a gunnery officer: "You may fire when you are ready, Gridley." Less than a year before, an editorial in Harper's Weekly characterized the United States Navy as "an asylum for old age and a grave for youthful ambition."

A huge triumphal parade was organized by Philippine insurgents in celebration of Manila's surrender to American troops on Aug. 14, 1898.

Sectional feelings were buried as North and South supported McKinley.

That no person shall be deprived of life, liberty or property without due process of law; that private property shall not be taken for public use without just compensation; that in all criminal prosecutions the accused shall enjoy the right to a speedy and public trial; to be informed of the nature and cause of the accusation, to be confronted with the witnesses against him, to have compulsory process for obtaining witnesses in his favor, and to have the assistance of counsel for his defence; that excessive bail shall not be required, nor excessive fines imposed, nor cruel and unusual punishment inflicted; that no person shall be put twice in jeopardy for the same offence, or be compelled in any criminal case to be a witness against himself; that the right to be secure against unreasonable searches and seizures shall not be violated; that neither slavery nor involuntary servitude shall exist except as a punishment for crime; that no bill of attainder, or ex-post-facte law shall be passed; that no law shall be passed abridging the freedom of speech or of the press, or the rights of the people to peaceably assemble and petition the government for a redress of grievances; that no law shall be made respecting an establishment of religion, or prohibiting the free exercise thereof, and that the free exercise and enjoyment of religious profession and worship without discrimination or preference shall forever be allowed.

William McKinley

Fundamental democratic rights were spelled out by President McKinley in his recommendations for Philippine government.

Kaiser Wilhelm's secret designs upon the islands were frustrated.

Ratification of peace terms at the White House on April 11, 1899, marked the end of the Spanish empire in the Pacific and the Americas and emergence of the U.S. as a world power.

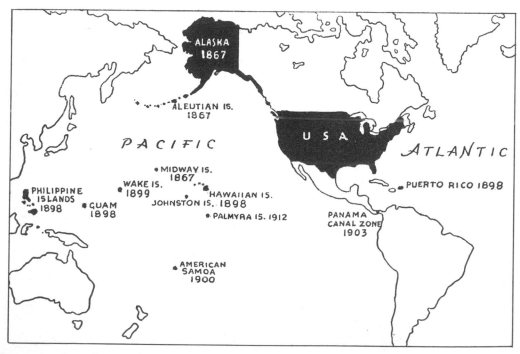

Expansion into the Pacific was greatly facilitated by the peace settlement. Spain ceded Puerto Rico, Guam, and the Philippines to the United States; Cuba secured its independence.

"The Cares of a Growing Family"—the above cartoon by Campbell Cory in the Sacramento Daily Bee—points up problems rising from the new colonial responsiblities of the United States.

Accompanied by President McKinley, Admiral George Dewey, the hero of Manila Bay, received the warm thanks of the nation at a ceremony held outside the Capitol on October 3, 1899.

On April 30, 1900, strategically important Hawaii became a full-fledged territory of the United States and citizenship privileges were conferred on its inhabitants. Fear of German and Japanese designs upon the islands and opposition to autocratic rule by Queen Liliuokalani contributed to annexation two years earlier at the urgings of natives as well as Americans.

News of Hawaii's union with the United States was greeted jubilantly in Honolulu.

Author of the "Open Door" policy adopted by the United States in the summer of 1900, John Hay, McKinley's Secretary of State, made notable contributions to world peace and stability. He promoted reciprocal trade agreements, supported the Hague Peace Conference of 1899, persuaded Germany, Britain, and Italy to settle their differences with Venezuela, prevailed upon Colombia to withdraw its objections to the Panama Canal and convinced Britain to submit Alaskan boundary disputes to arbitration.

Espousal of the "Open Door" policy induced the other great powers to guarantee the territorial integrity of China and stopped discriminatory practices in the treatment of trade with that country.

It was with some skepticism that McKinley chose Theodore Roosevelt as running mate in 1900.

Delegates to the Philadelphia convention of June 1900; note Roosevelt seated in the front row.

For President — For Vice President

WM. McKINLEY — THEO. ROOSEVELT

Unanimously renominated, McKinley seemed certain of reelection with Theodore Roosevelt on his ticket, but the competition of seven other parties (Democratic, Prohibition, People's, Social Democratic, Social Labor, United Christian, Union Reform) presented unexpected complications.

Tempers rose when McKinley supporters encountered Bryan men during campaign parades.

The sectional character of the campaign is pointed up by the above caricature depicting Bryan's followers as western savages seeking war with pro-McKinley east.

With prices low and wages relatively high, the average voter was inclined to be skeptical about Democratic promises of greater prosperity under Bryan. Note prices in the grocery list on the right.

"Don Quixote" Bryan met disaster decisively in his second tilt with the Republican "Full Dinner Pail". McKinley was reelected President by a greater majority than that of 1896.

271

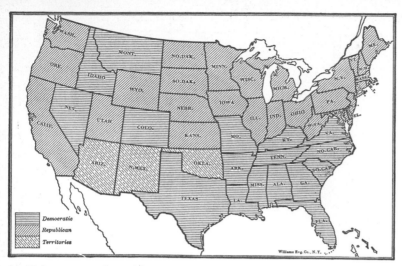

McKinley was reelected by the largest Republican plurality since 1872.

New Yorkers who supported McKinley went wild when news of his reelection was received.

espite the inclement weather, McKinley's inauguration on March 4, 1901, was heavily attended.

Continuation of prosperity was the keynote of McKinley's address.

The inaugural ball was one of the gayest, most colorful in the history of the nation's capital.

Trade with other nations increased as a result of tariff reductions McKinley promised in his campaign. The Dingley Act of 1897 was amended and reciprocal arrangements urged.

Why should n't business-men enjoy a little spin while dictating to their typewriters?

Bicycle hair-cutting establishments ought to do a rushing business with wheeling enthusiasts.

The old style of sprinkling-carts will soon be superseded by something more popular.

What the President's hand-shaking receptions will soon develop into, at the rate the bicycle craze is growing.

Cooks could, as well as not, get a little wheeling exercise while chopping hash.

The next thing that train-boys will offer to railroad travelers.

Bicycling was fast turning into a fad which threatened to upset social, business, and even political customs. "There's No Telling Where It Will Stop," Opper titled this cartoon.

275

Bustling Philadelphia was finding its streets too narrow for comfort.

Pullman travel, 1900 style, offered many of the pleasures of club life.

The discovery of gold in Alaska aroused the restless, young and old.

Fast-growing New York was already the world's second largest city.

Federal agents in Oklahoma when more Indian land was opened to settlement in 1901.

Competition for homestead claims was so great that it was decided to assign them by drawing lots. This prevented large family holdings and malpractices.

El Reno's Main Street several days before homesteaders invaded nearby territory.

They helped out when homestead lottery numbers were drawn at El Reno on July 29th.

Oklahoma was nicknamed the "Sooner State" because many of the best tracts had been surreptitiously staked out by settlers of 1889 in advance of the officially designated time.

Even standing room was scarce on the morning of the anxiously awaited lottery drawing.

A photo taken on August 6, 1901, near Lawton, Oklahoma, when another strip of public land was opened for settlement.

Above photo of McKinley with Secretary of Agriculture James L. Wilson (left) and James G. Milburn was taken shortly before the President was shot while visiting Buffalo's Pan-American Exposition on Sept. 6, 1901. On hand were Marcus Hanna (left below) and other advisers.

Rushing up to McKinley during a public reception at the Buffalo exposition, anarchist Leon Czolgoz fired two shots from a revolver hidden in a handkerchief. After hovering between life and death for eight days, McKinley succumbed at two a.m. on September 14, 1901.

The youngest American to occupy the White House (he was 42 when he succeeded McKinley in 1901), Theodore Roosevelt was also the first Republican President from the East. In all things he was indefatigable—in combatting his handicaps as a youngster afflicted by asthma and extreme near-sightedness, in the strenuous exercise he took to develop his frail body into a magnificent physique, in preparing a history of the War of 1812 while he was still a Harvard undergraduate, in getting himself elected to the New York legislature at 23, in running for Mayor of New York City at 28, in serving as a Civil Service Commissioner (1889-1895), in combatting crime as Police Commissioner of New York City (1895-1897), in modernizing the Navy while he was Assistant Secretary of the Navy (1897-1898), in organizing and leading the "Rough Riders" during the Spanish-American War (1898), in instituting far-reaching reforms during his Governorship of New York State (1898-1900), in campaigning for the Vice Presidency (1900), and in advancing the domestic and international interests of the United States during his Presidency

The above sketches show T. R. as cowboy, historian, Police Commissioner of New York City, Assistant Secretary of the Navy, and Rough Rider of the Spanish-American War. Below he is seen as Governor of New York, Vice President, President, Nobel Prize Winner, and Hunter Extraordinary.

At right is a photo of T. R. decked out in boxing garb during his undergraduate days at Harvard. Although sickly as a youngster, he developed a striking physique through exercise and outdoor life.

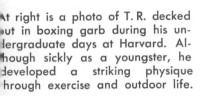

Roosevelt (left) at 22 with his brother Elliott.

Rancher of the Dakotas.

Pictured as a dude when he entered politics, T. R. was viewed skeptically.

While in the New York legislature, Roosevelt introduced reform bills supported by Grover Cleveland and opposed by the "Old Guard" Republicans.

Roosevelt addressing a street audience with characteristic gestures. "I preach to you, my countrymen, that our country calls not for the life of ease, but for the life of strenuous endeavor," he told a flag day audience. "Nothing in this world is worth having or worth doing unless it means effort, pain, difficulty . . . Let us therefore boldly face the life of strife."

Unique among American Presidents for the variety of his activities and interests, T.R. was undoubtedly in the limelight more often than any other head of a nation during his lifetime. "A man who could do so much could not do everything perfectly, though few have ever done so many things so well," observed historian Albert Bushnell Hart. "It was more true of him than of most men that his defects were inherent in his virtues. There were few half-tones in Roosevelt's moral perceptions and fewer in his vocabulary; he saw things as either black or white, and he forgot sometimes that he had not previously seen them as he saw them at the moment . . . The very intensity of his convictions sometimes blinded him to the sincerity and even to the justice of other points of view. Nevertheless, this intensity, this moral fervor, gave his ideas a momentum and a success which they could never have acquired had they proceeded from a more judicial mind. He scorned 'weasel words', and on occasion he did not hesitate to describe his enemies as thieves and liars. His remarkable energy reminded observers of some great elemental force which, like any natural phenomenon, is controlled by its own necessary laws." In the course of his crowded and many-sided life, Roosevelt wrote some 37 books on history, politics, military affairs, travel, exploration, and nature. Among the colorful expressions he coined were "lunatic fringe", "bull moose", "weasel words" and "my hat is in the ring".

An intensely devoted family man, Roosevelt was so shocked by the death of his first wife (less than three years after their marriage) and of his mother within a few hours of each other on February 10, 1884, that he retired to the private life of a North Dakota ranchman for two years. In 1887 he married Edith Kermit Carow (right), a childhood friend. By his first wife he had one daughter, Alice; by his second he had four sons (Theodore, Jr., Kermit, Archie, and Quentin and a daughter, Ethel). Below is T.R. with the second Mrs. Roosevelt and their children. "As I mounted the White House steps," Roosevelt reminisced about events of 1904, "Edith came to meet me, and I suddenly realized that, no matter what the outcome of the election, my happiness was assured, for my life with Edith and my children constitutes my happiness."

Lieut. Col. Roosevelt with his famous "Rough Riders". When war with Spain was declared, he resigned as Assistant Secretary of the Navy and helped organize the First U.S. Volunteer Cavalry.

DRAWING
THE LINE
IN MISSISSIPPI

Berryman 1902

The Teddy Bear vogue followed the appearance of this cartoon by Clifford Berryman. In the course of a hunting trip in Mississippi with Berryman, Roosevelt refused to shoot a small bear. The public saw in the episode a quality it liked to associate with Roosevelt's personality and toymakers quickly sensed a good thing. Overnight the Teddy Bear became immortal.

An enthusiastic outdoor sportsman since his college days, Roosevelt seldom lost an opportunity to go hunting. The above photograph shows him with a rhinoceros he bagged in Africa. He is seen below with guides and his son Kermit, a frequent companion.

"When the News of President Roosevelt's Visit Reached Africa", a cartoon by John T. McCutcheo

Teddy in Berlin

Teddy in Norway

Teddy in Holland

Teddy in Italy

Teddy in Budapest

Teddy in London

Teddy in Vienna

The indelible impressions T.R. made during his travels evoked these delightful drawings by Gruelle in the Cleveland Press. He surprised Europeans with his encyclopedic knowledge of their history and customs. However, some old world peculiarities startled him. At a royal dinner party in Rome he found that his hat was not taken from him until after he had escorted the Queen to the table.

Teddy in Paris

"He's Good Enough For Me", a famous cartoon by Homer Davenport.

Mark Hanna's memory was honored by the Chicago convention of June 1904; he died earlier in the year. Roosevelt, whom Hanna once referred to as "that damned cowboy", was unanimously nominated for a full term of his own. The Democrats chose Judge Alton B. Parker as their candidate. In a campaign speech at Jackson, Michigan, on the occasion of the fiftieth anniversary of the "under the oaks" convention, Secretary of State John Hay called attention to the nation's immense growth since the founding of the party: "Fourteen new states have entered the Union. The census of 1850 gave us 23,000,000 of population—the last one 76,000,000. The number of our farms — the total of our cultivated acreage — has increased fourfold. Our corn crop is five times what it was; our wheat crop, six times. The capital invested in manufacturing has grown from five hundred millions to ten billions; where it employed less than a million artisans, it now employs more than five millions; and while the number of workingmen has increased five times, their wages have increased tenfold. The value of manufactured property is thirteen times what it was . . . The real and personal wealth of the country has grown in this amazing half century from seven thousand millions to ninety-four thousand millions. Our railroads have grown from a mileage of sixteen thousand to one of two hundred thousand. Our imports and exports have gone up by leaps and bounds to the same proportions."

Roosevelt's "Prosperity Special" contrasted with hard times under **Grover Cleveland.**

These posters pointed up the theme "Don't give the Democrats another chance."

"President Roosevelt Has Built the Road Leading Directly to the White House."

"The Rip Van Winkle Awakening of Democracy", a cartoon by Albert Weil.

Senator Charles W. Fairbanks (right) was chosen Roosevelt's running mate in 1904.

Their platform stressed G.O.P. accomplishments and Democratic shortcomings.

"No people on earth have more cause to be thankful than ours," Roosevelt declared in his inaugural speech of March 5, 1905, "and this is said reverently, in no spirit of boastfulness in our own strength, but with gratitude to the Giver of Good, who has blessed us with the conditions which have enabled us to achieve so large a measure of well-being and happiness . . . But justice and generosity in a nation, as in an individual, count most when shown not by the weak but by the strong. While ever careful to refrain from wronging others, we must be no less insistent that we are not wronged ourselves. We wish peace; but we wish the peace of justice, the peace of righteousness. We wish it because we think it is right, and not because we are afraid. No weak nation that acts rightly and justly should ever have cause to fear, and no strong power should ever be able to single us out as a subject for insolent aggression . . . Our relations with the other powers of the world are important; but still more important are our relations among ourselves. Such growth in wealth, in population, and in power, as a nation has seen during a century and a quarter of its national life, is inevitably accompanied by a like outgrowth in the problems which are ever before every nation that rises to greatness. Power invariably means both responsibility and danger. Our forefathers faced certain perils which we have outgrown. We now face other perils the very existence of which it was impossible that they should foresee." Roosevelt was escorted to the Capitol by Rough Riders.

"The Great American Durbar" pictured Roosevelt's inauguration for Harper's Weekly readers.

A photograph montage of a Cabinet session (right to left around the table): President Roosevelt; George B. Cortelyou, Secretary of the Treasury; Charles J. Bonaparte, Attorney General; Victor H. Metcalf, Secretary of the Navy; James Wilson, Secretary of Agriculture; Oscar S. Straus, Secretary of Commerce and Labor; James R. Garfield, Secretary of the Interior; George Von L. Meyer, Postmaster General; William Howard Taft, Secretary of War; Elihu Root, Secretary of State. Attorney General Bonaparte was a grandson of Jerome Bonaparte, Napoleon's brother.

As these cartoons suggest, trust-busting was one of Roosevelt's favorite indoor sports. Although he repeatedly emphasized his friendship toward business and his opposition to government ownership, he early made it clear that he would not tolerate illegal monopolies and combinations in restraint of interstate trade. In his very first message to Congress he devoted much attention to railroad and trust questions. While conceding that large aggregates of capital could not be prevented and were even desirable under certain conditions, he took the position that big business should be subject to regulation, investigation, and, when necessary, prosecution. Shortly thereafter he proceeded to revitalize the Sherman Anti-Trust Act by instituting proceedings against the powerful Northern Securities Company on the ground that it constituted a monopoly of transportation in the northwest. The Supreme Court's decision against the company in 1904 was regarded by Roosevelt as one of the "great achievements" of his administration. Subsequently suits were launched against monopolies in coal, oil, tobacco, powder, and other commodities.

303

Improvement of working conditions and industrial expansion were fostered through the establishment of the United States Department of Commerce and Labor as a Cabinet agency in 1903.

Spurred by Roosevelt's recommendations, New York and other states adopted laws forbidding the employment of women and minors in industry under unsafe and unsanitary conditions.

As Chief Chemist of the U.S. Department of Agriculture, Harvey W. Wiley (center) laid the groundwork for present-day food and drug regulation. His pioneer efforts persuaded T.R. to advocate and obtain passage of the Meat Inspection and Pure Food and Drug Acts of 1906. Designed to prevent adulteration and misbranding, these measures prohibited interstate commerce of food and drugs containing deleterious ingredients. Proper labelling was also required.

With the advice and assistance of these conservation experts, Roosevelt drew up a far-reaching program for the protection of the nation's fast dwindling natural resources. Next to corporate monopolies, conservation was in his opinion "the most vital internal question of the United States."

The establishment of five more national parks and fifteen new national monuments stimulated travel as well as keener appreciation of America's heritage. Seen above is a tourist at Grand Canyon.

Accompanied by famed naturalist John Muir (the thickly bearded gentleman at the right), Roose-velt visited Yosemite National Park in the summer of 1903. Muir advised T.R. on conservation.

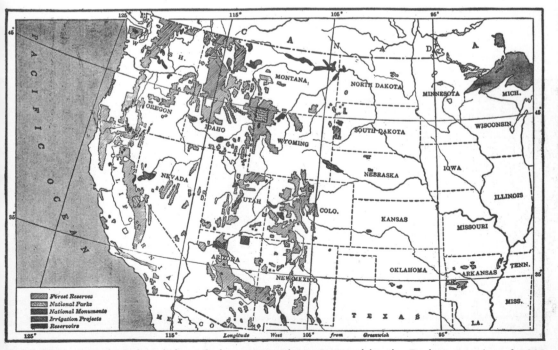

Redemption of neglected and despoiled western soil was initiated by the Reclamation Act of 1902. The area of natural forests was increased by over 140,000,000 acres by the new Bureau of Forestry.

A photograph of homestead applicants standing outside the U.S. Land Office bureau in Yank-town, S.D. The Kinkaid Bill enacted by Congress in 1904 liberalized federal public land grants.

A line-up at the U. S. Land Office in Vancouver, Washington. Nearby timber land was offered to settlers. Enlarged homesteads were authorized by a series of laws Roosevelt recommended.

"An Impregnable Shield", by Ole May in the Pittsburgh Gazette-Times.

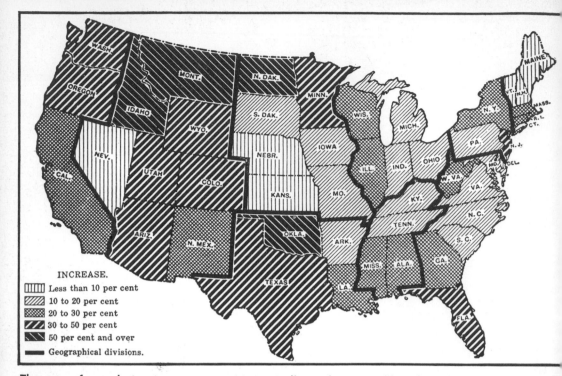

INCREASE.

||||| Less than 10 per cent
/// 10 to 20 per cent
▓▓▓ 20 to 30 per cent
▨▨▨ 30 to 50 per cent
\\\ 50 per cent and over
■■■ Geographical divisions.

The rate of population increase was rising rapidly in the west although concentrations remaine◄ highest in the east. When the thirteenth census was taken in 1910, the population of the natio◄ was 91,972,266—almost four times the number of persons in the U.S. in 1854.

RISE AND FALL OF IMMIGRATION

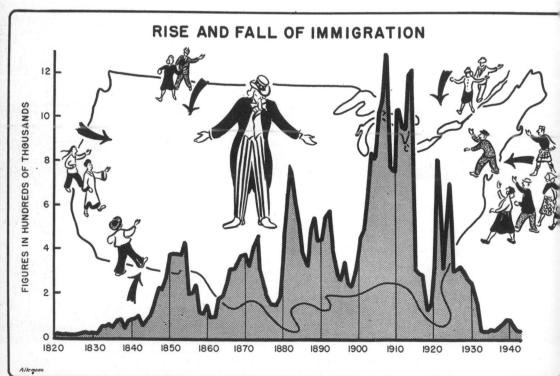

FIGURES IN HUNDREDS OF THOUSANDS

12

10

8

6

4

2

0

1820 1830 1840 1850 1860 1870 1880 1890 1900 1910 1920 1930 1940

Alkemono

As the above chart shows, immigration to the United States reached its peak in the years 1900-1910.

"The Steerage," a photograph Alfred Stieglitz took at Ellis Island, N.Y., in 1907. No President had a keener appreciation than Roosevelt of the extent to which America is an amalgam of foreign nationalities. His ancestors were Dutch, English, Scotch, Irish, French, and German.

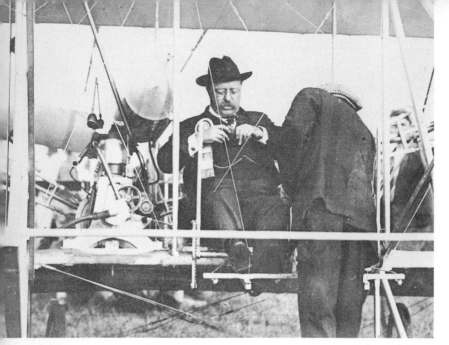

The father of American military aviation, T.R. was an early flying enthusiast. He took a keen personal interest in the experiments of the Wright brothers and encouraged purchase from them of the first airplane used by the national government. He is seen preparing to make an ascent in 1910.

The Army's first airplane en route to Fort Myer, Va., for its initial demonstration by the Wrights.

When the Army's first airplane made this trial flight, Orville Wright was at the controls.

At left is Orville Wright supervising the unloading of the plane he and his brother constructed expressly for the Army.

Army officers at Fort Sam Houston tested the Wright airplane for reconnaissance use.

Alarmed by reports that the Japanese government was making secret preparations for war against the United States, Roosevelt advised Secretary of State Elihu Root on July 13, 1907: "I am more concerned over the Japanese situation than any other. Thank Heaven we have our Navy in good shape." It was this "situation" which inspired a two-year (1907 - 1909) 'round - the - world cruise by 16 battleships with 12,000 men and officers. Major purpose of the trip was to impress Japan with American strength. In his autobiography, Roosevelt referred to his action in this connection as "the most important service that I rendered to peace." The importance of sea power was so plainly evident when the fleet returned that Congress increased naval appropriations substantially.

"Ain't It a Daisy?"—a Philadelphia Record cartoon.

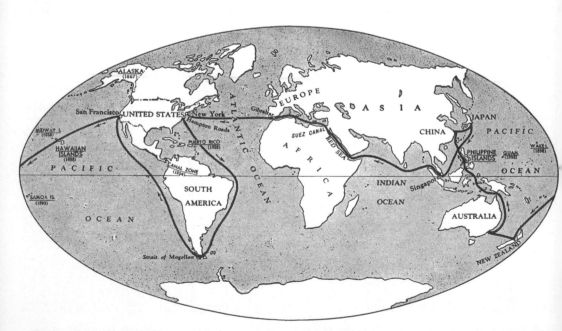

Route of the 1907-1909 Navy trip around the world; the great powers were much impressed.

A strong believer in preparedness for every eventuality, Roosevelt was chiefly responsible for the rise of the United States as a major military power. He greatly increased, through encouragement and appropriations, the efficiency of both the Army and the Navy. At his insistence young officers became eligible for promotion by virtue of merit without exclusive regard to the traditional rules of seniority. As Assistant Secretary of the Navy during McKinley's first administration, T.R. contributed to the modernization of the Navy and the defeat of Spain's Asiatic fleet in the Spanish-American War. His history of the War of 1812, written while he was an undergraduate at Harvard, prophetically called attention to the future importance of sea power.

War with militaristic Japan seemed inevitable to Roosevelt.

A 1902 photo of the Navy's first submarine, the U.S.S. Holland, its crew, and several visitors.

A painting of the construction of the Miraflores lock of the Panama Canal. Endorsed by the Republican platform of 1900 as vital to American defense and commerce, the canal became a reality largely through Roosevelt's efforts. Excavation on a large scale was not begun until 1906.

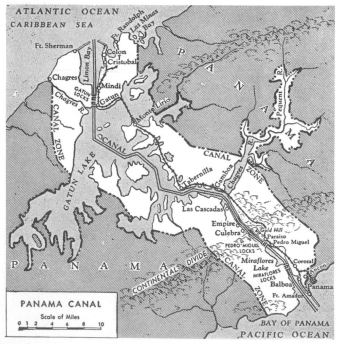

When Congressional procrastination threatened the project, Roosevelt became impatient. "I took the Canal Zone," he boasted, "and let Congress debate, and while the debate goes on, the canal does so also." It took three years of preliminary work and seven years of digging to complete the fifty-mile waterway. As of the end of 1953, tolls paid for the use of the canal were double the original cost of $380 million.

In visiting the canal in 1908, T.R. upset the precedent which was supposed to prevent a President from leaving the territory of the U.S. during his term of office. He is seen at the Culberra Cut.

Convinced of the strategic need of the waterway during the Spanish-American War and sensing the vital part the Pacific was destined to play, both politically and commercially, in world history, T.R. took swift and vigorous action to build the canal. The water distance between the east and west coasts of the United States was reduced by 8,000 miles. Passage between the Atlantic and Pacific Oceans became a matter of hours instead of weeks. Construction of the canal constituted an unparalleled engineering feat.

T.R. with the Russian and Japanese envoys at the historic peace conference of 1905 in Portsmouth, New Hampshire. Left to right are Count
Witte, Baron Rosen, Roosevelt, Minister Takahira, and Baron Komura.

In prevailing upon Russia and Japan to end their long drawn out war,
Roosevelt won the respect and gratitude of a troubled world. The peace
treaty was signed on September 5th after many delays and difficulties.

"Teddy in a New Role", a cartoon the Newark Evening News ran when Roosevelt let it be known that the $37,000 Nobel Peace Award he received in 1906 would be used to promote arbitration of labor disputes.

Inter-American friendship was firmly cemented by Roosevelt and Secretary of State Elihu Root at the cornerstone ceremonies at the Pan American Union building in Washington in May 1908. Facing T.R. at the left are Cardinal Gibbons, Andrew Carnegie, Root, and John Barrett.

The Roosevelt policy of "speaking softly" and "carrying a big stick" paid dividends in making possible the Panama Canal despite difficulties with adjoining nations, in discouraging German aggression toward Venezuela, in settling disputes with Great Britain over Alaska's boundary, in bringing an end to Russo-Japanese hostilities, in staving off war between the U.S. and Japan, and in promoting the International Court of Arbitration. In accepting the Nobel Peace Award, he delivered an address in which he proposed the prevention of war and the maintenance of peace through a world organization similar to that of the United Nations in many essential respects.

When France and Germany quarreled over Morocco in 1907, T.R. insisted they settle their differences peacefully.

The position of the United States in world affairs was greatly strengthened by T.R. Although two notable Secretaries of State, John Hay and Elihu Root, served under him, he played a major role in the formulation of foreign policies. "He knew the involutions of international politics in the Old World as no American President had known them," according to Hermann Hagedorn, "and he countered and checked his subtle opponents in diplomacy with skill and relish. He was bold — startling bold at times — but never reckless . . . He found the government of the U.S. in the position among world powers of a new boy in school; he left it firmly established in the first rank."

Roosevelt used his needle effectively in persuading Nicaragua, Salvador, and Honduras to get along amicably

"I would rather see Elihu Root in the White House than any other man now possible," Roosevelt confided to a friend as the election of 1908 drew near. "I would walk on my hands and knees from the White House to the Capitol to see Root made President. But I know it cannot be done. He couldn't be elected." One of the most brilliant statesmen in American history, Root rendered distinguished service as Secretary of War in McKinley's cabinet and as Secretary of State under T.R. He reorganized the War Department, created the General Staff, improved the State Department's consular service, promoted better relations with Latin America, and concluded arbitration treaties with the major powers. Like Roosevelt, he also received the Nobel Prize in recognition of his efforts in behalf of international peace. He was closely identified with G.O.P. reform elements.

The American way of life permitted more time for fun at the beach, leisurely outdoor concerts,

and visits to amusement parks offering irresistible pleasures to children and the young in heart.

"I think Taft has the most lovable personality I have ever come in contact with," Theodore Roosevelt once said to a White House aide. Many people who knew William Howard Taft felt pretty much the same way about him. His friendliness, like his sense of humor, was infectious. Unlike Roosevelt, he was undramatic, predictable, and conciliatory. The son of a member of Grant's cabinet, he was educated at Yale, and entered public service after a brief stint as a lawyer in Cincinnati, where he was born in 1857. He rose steadily from post to post—Prosecuting Attorney, County Solicitor, Judge of Ohio's Superior Court, Solicitor General of the United States, Judge of the Federal Circuit Court, President of the Philippine Commission, Governor of the Philippines, Secretary of War, and Trouble-Shooter Extraordinary for President Roosevelt. Mark Sullivan summed up his qualities this way: "Wherever a tension needed the solvent of good will, or friction the oil of benevolence, wherever suspicion needed the antidote of frankness or wounded pride the disinfectant of a hearty laugh—there Taft was sent." It was at least partly for these reasons that T.R. favored Taft as his successor—only to have a change of heart several years later.

A 1909 photograph of President Taft with sons Charles and Robert.

Mr. and Mrs. Taft with their sons and daughter Helen. Despite opposition from supporters of his famed brother, Charles (left), a social reformer, won the Republican nomination for Governor of Ohio in 1952.

The first President to enjoy a White House car, Taft often rode with his family.

A family reunion in 1921 brought together Robert (left), Charles (right), Helen (top row, right) and son-in-law Frederick Manning (top row, extreme right) with their children. Harding appointed William H. Taft Chief Justice of the United States.

"Why don't you speak for yourself, John", a cartoon Joseph Keppler drew for Puck in 1908. Loc
to take a back seat in national affairs, T.R. expected to wield influence in Washington through To

"The Fortune Teller" (left) appeared in the Pittsburgh Sun and "Blind (?) Man's Buff" in the Chica
Daily News. As the latter cartoon suggests, T.R. didn't care to be succeeded by Secretary of Sta
Elihu Root, Vice President Charles W. Fairbanks, Senator Albert Beveridge or Senator Joseph Forake

"The Important Introduction", a New York Mail cartoon by Homer Davenport suggestive of his well-known "He's Good Enough For Me" drawing about T.R.

From the porch of his brother's home in Cincinnati, Taft announced he would continue Roosevelt's policies. He is seen addressing friends and well wishers on June 20, 1908, the day he was formally notified he had been chosen as the standard bearer of the Republican Party. His nomination was made by fellow Ohioan Warren Gamaliel Harding.

At the left is "De-light-ed," a Brooklyn Daily Eagle cartoon by Nelson Harding.

We demand immediate tariff revision and believe in a free interchange of products between the United States and the Philippines except in sugar and tobacco. We favor establishment of postal savings banks. We agree to laws preventing overissue of stocks and bonds on railroads, etc. We promise a safety legislation for labor.

We promise a plan to enlarge the uses of inland water ways and harbors. We advise a safeguard to public health. We desire a national bureau of mines and mining. We will stop at once the accumulation of dishonest wealth, thereby carefully distributing the national wealth more fairly.

With James S. Sherman, a popular New York Congressman, as his running mate, Taft campaigned vigorously. Their platform called for lower tariffs, regulation of stocks and bonds, safety legislation for labor, postal savings banks, and checks on "the accumulation of dishonest wealth".

"In history," declared the Resolutions Committee of the 1908 convention, "the difference between Democracy and Republicanism is that one stood for debased currency, the other for honest money; the one for free silver, the other for honest currency; the one for free trade, the other for protection; the one for the contraction of American influence, the other for expansion. One has been forced to abandon every position it has taken on the great issues before the people; the other has held and vindicated all. In experience the difference between Democracy and Republicanism is that the one means adversity, while the other means prosperity. One means low wages; the other means high wages. One means doubt and debt; the other means confidence and thrift."

THE G. O. P.

I

Stand by the G. O. P. boys, stand by the crowd,
Stand by the G. O. P. makes a nation strong and proud,
Stand by the G. O. P., our opponents they have split
And when the election's over they'l surely have a fit.

CHORUS.

Not without your wondrous story, G. O. P.,
Can be writ the nation's glory, G. O. P.,
On the record of the years
Abraham Lincoln's name appears,
McKinley, Logan and our tears, G. O. P.

II

Stand by the G. O. P., Teddy and his nag,
Stand by the G. O. P. our opponents we will bag,
Stand by the stars and stripes that wave so clear and
bright,
They'll carry the nation's problems thro' the darkest
night.

A campaign song written by Lewis T. Watkins.

331

Wired for sound, campaign innovations included phonograph records widely distributed by party workers at nominal cost.

"Certain of his election", a Homer Davenport cartoon in the New York Evening Mail.

Both had much in common in 1908. Taft won the election with 50,000 more votes than Roosevelt received in 1904; he defeated Bryan, T.R.'s rival in the previous campaign, with a popular majority of a million and a quarter votes.

"Alone I Didn't Do It", a cartoon by Bernard Partridge in the London weekly, Punch.

President-elect Taft and his predecessor arriving at the Capitol on March 4, 1909. Because of freezing temperature, swearing-in ceremonies were held in the Senate Chamber.

Accompanied by Mrs. Taft, the beaming new President headed the inaugural parade in an open carriage despite the inclement weather. Note "bowlers" on Secret Service men.

Flanked by Vice President James S. Sherman (left) and Edward Hallwagon, chairman of the inaugural committee (right), Taft reviewed the inaugural parade in high spirits.

Top-hatted Charles Evans Hughes, then New York's Governor, cut an impressive figure in the parade. In the following year Taft appointed him to the Supreme Court.

Vice President Sherman attained prominence as the acknowledged leader of New York Republicans. He served in the House of Representatives almost continuously from 1887 to 1909.

Irascible House Speaker "Uncle Joe" Cannon, Taft's strong right arm in Congress, fought a losing battle against party insurgents even after he came out in support of lower tariffs.

Taft with his Cabinet (left to right, around the table): President Taft; Franklin MacVeagh, Secretary of the Treasury; George W. Wickersham, Attorney General; George Von L. Meyer, Secretary of the Navy; James Wilson, Secretary of Agriculture; Charles Nagel, Secretary of Commerce and Labor; Walter L. Fisher, Secretary of the Interior; Frank H. Hitchcock, Postmaster General; Henry L. Stimson, Secretary of War; Philander C Knox, Secretary of State.   A 1912 photograph.

Taft visiting with Cardinal James Gibbons and Governor Hughes at Cliff Haven, New York, in 1909.

Roosevelt Dam, then the world's l a r g e s t, was dedicated by its name-sake in the fall of 1911.

Approval of the Arizona Statehood Bill in 1912 brought the forty-eighth state into the Union.

"Good Political Economy", a cartoon by John T. McCutcheon, signified popular approval of reforms Taft instituted. During his administration a creditable record was built up undramatically. Postal savings banks were created. Suits were brought against forty-five trusts. The Sixteenth Amendment, authorizing taxation of income, was adopted; the Seventeenth, calling for the direct election of Senators, was submitted to the States. The Interstate Commerce Commission was strengthened appreciably by the Mann-Elkins Act. Future candidates for Congress and the Presidency were required by law to make public their campaign expenditures. On March 4, 1913, Taft's last day in office, he signed the act which established the Department of Labor with a cabinet officer

"Design For a White House Suited to Present Day Needs" was the title of this delightful cartoon.

FIRST IN AMERICA
AVIATION MEET
LOS ANGELES
JANUARY 10-20 1910
American & Foreign Aviators
DAILY FLIGHTS

The nation looked skyward with amazement and some apprehension.

A meeting of the old and new left little doubt as to the need for federal support of public roads.

Bursting at the seams, Chicago was growing faster than New York in commerce and population.

Roosevelt's interest in a third cup of Presidential coffee didn't completely surprise Taft as the 1912 elections approached. The two drifted apart gradually but discernibly after 1910. T.R. felt his successor had let him down by not continuing the "Square Deal". Taft, on the other hand, felt T.R. had no right to expect him to be a rubber-stamp occupant of the White House.

Taft: "Eyes front!"—an Art Young cartoon published on the eve of the national convention.

Badly split by the division between Roosevelt and Taft, the party seemed to be on the verge of dismemberment when the national convention of 1912 assembled. After obtaining control of the convention machinery through methods challenged by Roosevelt delegates, Taft's supporters crushed T.R.'s candidacy with steam roller thoroughness that pleased the New York Times (note cartoon below) and other leading papers. Taft was renominated on the first ballot. Roosevelt bolted the party to run on the Progressives' "Bull Moose" ticket with Senator Hiram Johnson of California as running mate.

"For Auld Lang Syne", a British interpretation of the battle between Roosevelt and Taft. When the smoke cleared and the ballots were counted, T.R. remarked ruefully, "There's only one thing to do and that is to go back to the Republican Party." This he did.

Scholarly Nicholas Murray Butler, seen above in a photograph taken after his retirement as President of Columbia University in 1945, became Taft's running mate when Vice Presidential candidate James S. Sherman died shortly before the November election.

"The End of the Campaign" by E. W. Kemble. While the Republican elephant and the Progressive bull moose trounced each other to exhaustion, the Democratic donkey ran off with the election of 1912.

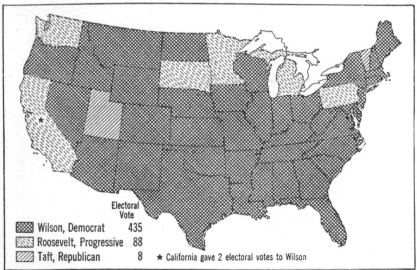

	Electoral Vote	
Wilson, Democrat	435	
Roosevelt, Progressive	88	
Taft, Republican	8	★ California gave 2 electoral votes to Wilson

The split in Republican ranks put a Democrat in the White House for the first time in sixteen years and the second time since 1860. Woodrow Wilson won the election with a popular vote even smaller than that Bryan received four years earlier. Roosevelt's vote of 4.1 millions and Taft's 3.4 millions totalled about a million and a half more than Wilson polled.

The first nominee for the Presidency to be genuinely drafted, Charles Evans Hughes, one of the most brilliant public servants in American history, undoubtedly would have won the election of 1916 if he had not lost California's electoral vote by a small margin because of an unintentional snub of powerful Senator Hiram Johnson. Born in Glen Falls, New York, on April 11, 1862, Hughes displayed precociousness as a child. At four he could read the Bible in English; at eight he read it in Greek. His college education began at 14 and he graduated from Brown University at the age of 19. Subsequently he studied law at Columbia University, entered private practice, and soon became known as a "lawyer's lawyer". So far as the public was concerned, however, he was a nobody when, in 1905, he was appointed counsel to a legislative committee investigating New York gas rates. His masterful work in this connection led to his selection, later that year, as the state's attorney for an investigation of insurance malpractices. He became a hero overnight and, in the words of President Taft, "the Republican Party's greatest asset." Such was his popularity that by 1906, less than two years after he had emerged from obscurity, he was nominated for the Governorship of New York on the Republican ticket. The only G.O.P. candidate for state office to survive a Democratic landslide, he defeated journalist William Randolph Hearst in a hotly fought campaign. At the end of his second term as Governor, he was appointed to the Supreme Court by Taft. It was with extreme reluctance that he resigned from the court in 1916 to run against Woodrow Wilson for the Presidency.

Hughes with his parents in an 1867 photo.

An avid reader of Shakespeare at 8.

A sophomore at Madison College at 14.

A graduate of Brown University at 19.

An adoring, fun-loving father and husband, Hughes spent most of his meager leisure with his family. He enjoyed reading "Mr. Dooley" and "Uncle Remus" to his children and writing whimsical rhymes for their birthdays. The executive mansion in Albany became a distinctly informal place when the Hughes family moved into it. Orphans from the nearby St. Joseph's Catholic Home were constant visitors; some were close friends of the Governor's daughters. Disregarding the special privileges of her new status, Mrs. Hughes ran the mansion like a typical American home. She rose at seven each morning to get the children off to school, worked through the day like most housewives, and assembled her family for dinner promptly at eight every evening. A white bull terrier was often permitted to sit on a chair close to the table during meal-time. The above photo shows Mr. and Mrs. Hughes with their daughters and only son.

Antoinette Carter became Hughes' "court of first and last resort" in 1883.

Their devotion never wavered during the 57 years of their life together.

"As an investigator," commented a World's Work writer, "Mr. Hughes has no enemies and no friends; one felt that even though his revelations were to affect his closest relatives, he still would not hesitate. He uncovered facts that reverberated the world over, almost without displaying a sense of personal triumph; he never browbeat witnesses, never threatened, hardly ever lifted his voice above the conversational tone." But when his indignation was aroused, it was quite devastating. Once an insurance company officer tried to justify extravagant expenditures by comparing them to fees paid to Hughes as a corporation lawyer. "My fees, sir," Hughes declared as he shot a long index finger under the witness' nose, "are not trust funds!"

"The Gridiron," a New York World cartoon of September 1905.

Hughes at work in his library during the period of his exposure of insurance malpractices.

velike, Hughes campaigned for Governor of New York with "magnificent eloquence" in 1906.

ghes' regime as Gov-
nor of New York was
tinguished by far-
aching reforms, in-
ding the regulation
public utilities, legis-
ion protecting wom-
and children in fac-
ies, stricter election
vs, and close super-
ion of race tracks.
is first act as Gover-
r," relates Irving
one, "was to move the
sk out of his private
ice into the large
uiting room, where
yone who had busi-
ss with him could
p right up and state
He made no swaps
bargains, but ap-
inted the best man he
uld find for each po-
ion, regardless of
rty. He was a mili-
nt crusader against
e abuses of trusts and
onopolies . . . His ef-
rts were always di-
cted against the abus-
, never against the
sinesses themselves."

A Hughes-for-Vice-President movement in 1908 had odd supporters.

Delegates to the Chicago convention of 1916 (above) drafted Hughes as the standard beare
of a reunited party despite his outspoken unwillingness to seek the nomination. "I hope," h
announced on the eve of the convention, "that as a justice of the Supreme Court I am rende
ing a public service and may continue to do so for many years; but the Supreme Court must n
be dragged into politics, and no man is as essential to his country's well-being as is the sustaine
integrity of the courts." Charles W. Fairbanks, Vice President under Roosevelt, was chosen
his running mate. In the bitter campaign that followed, Hughes was so badly smeared b
rumors that he was "pro-German" that his loyalty had to be played up as in the sign belov

As a Presidential candidate, Hughes launched a militant campaign to refute reports that he did not intend to fight for the office he had not sought. A month after he took to the road, the New York Post reported: "He is making one of the most remarkable records of successful campaigning of any Presidential candidate in recent years." Although Hughes and Wilson, the Democratic nominee, differed politically, they had remarkable similarities. Both were sons of clergymen; both had shown unusual abilities during childhood; both had been college professors; both had been progressive governors of their states; both had vigorously opposed monopolies; both were men of keen intellect; both were public servants rather than politicians.

Hughes spoke out vigorously for women's suffrage, wider extension of the federal merit syste efficiency in government, and a firmer stand with warring nations over the rights of America

Examples of the vilification Hughes was subjected to by cartoonists of opposition newspapers

Conferring with ex-President William H. Taft.

Visiting with his friend General Leonard Wood.

In his whistle stop speeches, Hughes used his wit and sharp legal mind to Democratic disadvantage.

Above: "The Lively Leader", a cartoon in the Washington, D. C., Evening Star. Below: Mrs. Hughes with her husband during his campaign.

FRED O SEIDEL

Assured of victory by election night returns, Hughes went to bed confident he had been chosen President. When he awoke the next morning he learned that, contrary to expectation, California had gone Democratic by a margin of several thousand votes; Wilson captured the Presidency by virtue of that state's electoral backing. One of the by-products of the campaign was the election of Jeanette Rankin, a Montana Republican, as the nation's first Congresswoman.

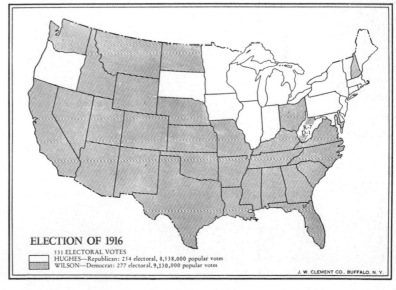

ELECTION OF 1916

531 ELECTORAL VOTES

HUGHES—Republican: 254 electoral, 8,538,000 popular votes
WILSON—Democrat: 277 electoral, 9,130,000 popular votes

J. W. CLEMENT CO., BUFFALO, N. Y.

The first person to be appointed twice to the Supreme Court, Hughes was named Chief Justice by President Hoover in 1930. He kept so close on the heels of the New Deal that President Franklin D. Roosevelt tried to expand the court in order to include more sympathetic members.

Although relatively obscure and one of the darkest of dark horses, Warren Gamaliel Harding was elected the nation's Chief Executive by a majority vote larger than that received by previous Presidential candidates. He was born November 2, 1865, on a farm near Blooming Grove, Ohio. The only son of a country doctor, he secured his education at Ohio Central College, entered journalism, and became the editor and owner of the Marion Star. His interest in local affairs led to participation in politics and, with the help of Senator Joseph B. Foraker, election to the Ohio legislature. After two terms in the State Senate, he became Lieutenant-Governor. Much to his own surprise, he won the U.S. Senatorial nomination away from Foraker in 1914, entered the upper chamber of Congress, and served in that body until he was chosen President in 1920.

Photographs by Herbert E. French.

Senator and Mrs. Harding in a photograph taken outside their Washington, D. C., home in 1920. The former Florence Kling, Mrs. Harding helped her husband develop the Marion Star into a leading Ohio newspaper and highly profitable business. In a moment of uneasiness about his health, she reportedly confided to a close friend: "I cannot see but one word written above his head if they make him President, and that word is 'tragedy'."

Harding was born November 8, 1865, in this farmhouse near Blooming Grove, Ohio.

With his two young sisters.

With his father, Dr. George Harding.

Relaxing on a golf course; he enjoyed the game and played it frequently in the summer.

Harding with Henry Ford and Thomas Alva Edison (front row, left) during a vacation visit.

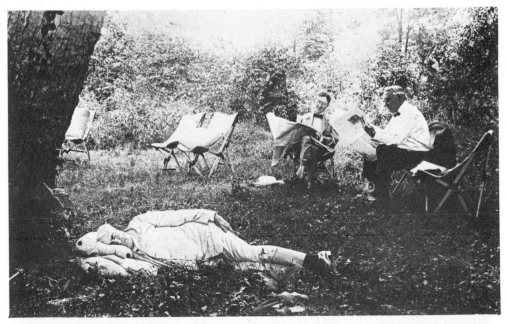

The gentleman in blissful repose at the left is inventor Edison; at the right is Harding.

Inconspicuous among these Senators departing for the Chicago convention of 1920 is Harding (fifth from the left). Standing to his right is Henry Cabot Lodge. The heavily mustached gentleman second from left is Charles Curtis, Vice President under Hoover. Harding was chosen the Party's compromise candidate on the tenth ballot.

Gen. Leonard Wood, rival for the 1920 nomination, paying his respects to Harding.

G.O.P. Chairman Will Hays, Harding, and running mate Calvin Coolidge. A shrewd Indiana lawyer with a keen sense for the nuances of public opinion, Hays put a great deal of new life into the party's organization. At his advice, Harding and Coolidge adopted a modified "front porch" campaign somewhat similar to that of McKinley.

Friendly to a fault, Harding was highly appreciative of support from his Ohio friends.

Shaking hands with William Jennings Bryan.

"America's present need," Harding declare in a Boston speech which seemed to sum u his philosophy, "is not heroics but healing not nostrums but normalcy, not revolutio but restoration, not agitation but adjustmen not experiment but equipoise, not submerg ence in internationality but sustainment i triumphant nationality." The party platform on which he stood favored reduction of th national debt, lower taxes, and flexible pro tective tariffs. It opposed membership i the League of Nations, but advocated "agreement among nations to preserve th peace . . . without compromising national in dependence." Isolationist sentiment wa strong in the west.

Like Harding, Democratic rival James M. Cox was an Ohioan who entered politics via journalism.

Senator Hiram Johnson fought vigorously for the Party's nomination in Chicago.

New York Tribune caricatures of personalities at the Republican convention of 1920 in Chicago.

Phonograph recordings of Harding's "front porch" speeches were widely distributed at the direction of Will Hays. Both friends and opponents were surprised by the popular appeal Harding attracted.

The rise of the Ku Klux Klan, movement aroused racial prejudices and animosities Harding deplored.

To the Men and Women of America

AN OPEN LETTER

When one citizen knows beyond the peradventure of doubt what concerns all other citizens but is not generally known, duty compels publication.

The father of Warren Gamaliel Harding is George Tryon Harding, second, now resident of Marion, Ohio, said to be seventy-six years of age, who practices medicine as a one-time student of the art in the office of Doctor McCuen, then resident in Blooming Grove, Morrow County, Ohio, and who has never been accepted by the people of Crawford, Morrow and Marion Counties as a white man.

Extract from an anonymously issued circular alleging that Harding had Negro blood; the New York Herald called it a "foul eleventh-hour attack." Democratic leaders repudiated the circular.

Extension of suffrage to women played an important part in the election results because a large number of mothers and wives were bitter about their losses in World War I and objected to American participation in the League of Nations. Harding charged the League was "conceived for world super-government, negotiated in misunderstanding, and intolerantly urged and demanded by its administration sponsors, who resisted every effort to safeguard America . . ."

Ratification of the Nineteenth Amendment, permitting women to participate in the 1920 election, inspired this Harry Westerman cartoon in the Ohio State Journal.

371

Crowds gathered in front of the White House on election night when the news services announced that Harding and Coolidge had won an easy victory with a popular vote of sixteen million to nine million for Democratic rivals James M. Cox and Franklin D. Roosevelt. "It wasn't a landslide," reportedly observed Joseph Tumulty, secretary to President Woodrow Wilson, "it was an earthquake."

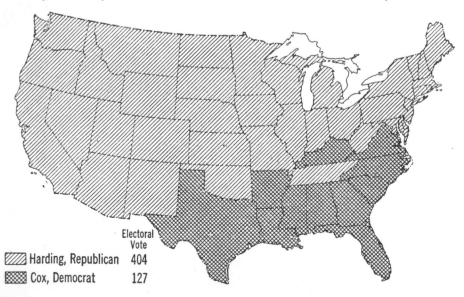

Electoral
Vote

Harding, Republican   404
Cox, Democrat   127

Thousands heard Harding declare at his inauguration on March 4, 1921: "I have taken the solemn oath of office on that passage of holy writ wherein it is asked 'What doth the Lord require but to do justly and to love mercy and walk humbly with my God?' This I plight to God and my country." The new President added: "We want to do our part in making offensive warfare so hateful that governments and people who resort to it must prove the righteousness of their cause or stand as outlaws before the bar of civilization . . . Today, better than ever before, we know the aspirations of mankind, and share them. We have come to a new realization of our place in the world and a new appraisal of our nation by the world. The unselfishness of these United States is a thing proven; our devotion to peace for ourselves and for the world is well established; our concern for preserved civilization has had its impassioned and heroic expression. There was no American failure to resist the attempted reversion of civilization; there will be no failure today or tomorrow . . . We want an America of homes, illumined with hope and happiness . . . we want to provide that no selfish interest, no material necessity, no lack of opportunity shall prevent the gaining of that education so essential to best citizenship."

In delivering his first address to Congress, President Harding urged conservative policies.

Vice President Coolidge exercising in the Senate gymnasium with House Speaker Gillette.

The Harding Cabinet. Seated, left to right, are John W. Weeks, Secretary of War; Andrew W. Mellon, Secretary of the Treasury; Charles Evans Hughes, Secretary of State; President Harding; Vice President Coolidge; Edwin Denby, Secretary of the Navy. Standing, left to right, are Albert B. Fall, Secretary of the Interior; Will Hays, Postmaster General; Harry M. Daugherty, Attorney General; Henry C. Wallace, Secretary of Agriculture; Herbert Hoover, Secretary of Commerce; James J. Davis, Secretary of Labor. Fall and Daugherty became involved in the Teapot Dome scandal which blighted Harding's short-lived administration.

Secretary of Labor James J. Davis with top officials of the Department of Labor in 1921.

"Now then, all together, 'My country, 'tis of thee'." A cartoon by Rollin Kirby in New York World.

Prohibition, enacted under Woodrow Wilson with Republican support, brought headaches, dissatisfaction and speakeasies in fairly rapid succession after Harding assumed the Presidency.

With youthful admirers from Pennsylvania.

With Albert Einstein and other scientists.

With Indians bearing gifts from Oklahoma.

With Coolidge and General John J. Pershing.

With baseball fans at the Griffith Stadium.

With Nobel Prize winner Madame Marie Curie.

"Drop It", a cartoon Rollin Kirby drew for the N. Y. World, symbolized post-war feeling here and abroad.

"No European Entanglements", a J. N. Ding caricature in the New York Tribune, reflected Republican policy.

Secretary of State Hughes welcoming delegates to the Washington Disarmament Conference of 1921-22, the most outstanding accomplishment of Harding's administration. Standing to Hughes' right is Aristide Briand, Premier of France; close to his left is General John J. Pershing.

President Harding addressing the opening session of the Disarmament Conference, held in the Pan American Union building. Although the Conference did not, as Secretary Hughes conceded, "absolutely end the race in competition in naval armaments," it led to a ten-year moratorium and a 5-5-3 power ratio more advantageous to the United States and Great Britain than to Japan.

Emissaries to the Washington disarmament parley were greatly impressed by Hughes' scheme for a ten-year moratorium on naval construction. He is seen above with Lyesato Tekugawa of Japan, Arthur Balfour of Great Britain, M. Briand of France, and Carlo Schauzer of Italy.

Destruction of heavy dreadnoughts convinced the world that America desired peace and had no imperialistic ambitions. Other nations followed suit, but Japan secretly prepared for war.

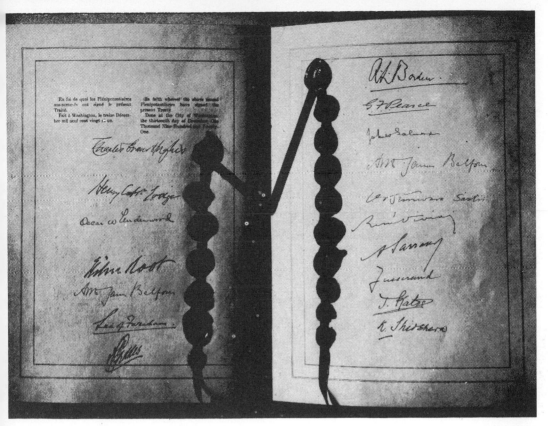

The Four-Power Treaty of 1921 dissolved the Anglo-Japanese military alliance and secured "respect" for U. S. rights in the Pacific. Treaty signers were Britain, Japan, France, and the U. S.

"Proof of the Pudding Is in Ratification", a cartoon in the Columbus Citizen of 1922.

A supporter of the World Court, Hughes found Senator Simeon Fess unsympathetic.

Chief Justice Taft, Harding, and Robert Todd Lincoln, son of the Civil War chief executive, at dedication of the Lincoln Memorial in Washington on May 31, 1922.

Taft delivered a memorable speech about Abe Lincoln at the monument ceremonies.

Among the significant achievements of Harding's short administration were the conclusion of peace treaties with Germany and Austria, establishment of the national budget system and of the General Accounting Office, strengthening of farm credit and cooperatives through the Capper-Volstead and Agricultural Credits Acts, introduction of equal pay for equal work in the civil service, and creation of the World War Foreign Debt Commission. However, these accomplishments were overshadowed when the Teapot Dome scandal and other irregularities came to light after Harding's death.

Close adviser to Harding on international affairs, Henry Cabot Lodge of Massachusetts held the strategic post of Chairman of the Senate's Foreign Relations Committee.

"Uncle Joe' Cannon, veteran member of Congress, left the House of Representatives in 1923—to relief of party insurgents and regret of old timers.

Leaving Washington on June 20, 1923, for their trip to Alaska.

President and Mrs. Harding in a photo taken when they arrived in Alaska. Although their relationship lacked warmth, rumors of marital difficulties seemed unjustified to their friends.

Scott Bone, Alaska's Governor, with President Harding.

Harding's body lying in state in the East Room of the White House. The President's sudden death upon his return from Alaska left the nation stunned. He died on August 3, 1923.

The New York Times.

VOL. LXXII...No. 23,932.   NEW YORK, FRIDAY, AUGUST 3, 1923.   TWO CENTS

PRESIDENT HARDING DIES SUDDENLY;
STROKE OF APOPLEXY AT 7:30 P. M.;
CALVIN COOLIDGE IS PRESIDENT

COOLIDGE TAKES THE OATH OF OFFICE

His Father, Who Is a Notary Public, Administers It After Form Is Found By Him in His Library.

ANNOUNCES HE WILL FOLLOW THE HARDING POLICIES

Wants All Who Aided Harding to Remain in Office—Roused After Midnight to Be Told the News of the President's Death.

Statement by President Coolidge

PLYMOUTH, Vt., Aug. 3.—President Calvin Coolidge issued the following statement early this morning:

Reports have reached me, which I fear are correct, that President Harding is gone. The world has lost a great and good man. I mourn his loss. He was my chief and my friend.

It will be my purpose to carry out the policies which he has begun for the service of the American people and for meeting their responsibilities wherever they may arise.

For this purpose I shall seek the cooperation of all those who have been associated with the President during his term of office.

Those who have given their efforts to assist him I wish to remain in office that they may assist me. I have faith that God will direct the destinies of our nation.

CALVIN COOLIDGE
Thirtieth President of the United States by the Death of President Harding

Public Men Voice Tributes

WARREN GAMALIEL HARDING
Twenty-ninth President of the United States, Who Died Yesterday in San Francisco

President's Death Shocks Capital.

DEATH STROKE CAME WITHOUT WARNING

Mrs. Harding Was Reading to Her Husband When First Sign Appeared —She Ran for Doctor

BUT NOTHING COULD BE DONE TO REVIVE PATIENT

News of Tragic End Shocks Everybody, Coming After Day Said to Have Been the Best Since His Illness Began a Week Ago.

SAN FRANCISCO, Aug. 3.—President Harding died at 7:30 o'clock tonight of a stroke of apoplexy.

Top portion of the black-leaded front page of the New York Times on August 3, 1923. For the sixth time, the nation mourned the death of a President during his term of office.

"Nothing human was alien to him," Secretary of State Hughes declared of Harding at a special memorial service held in the Capitol. Members of Congress and other notables heard Hughes' simple but eloquent eulogy. Among those seated in the first row are Herbert Hoover, Andrew Mellon, President Coolidge, and Chief Justice Taft.

When shy, tight-lipped, and frugal Calvin Coolidge assumed the vast burdens of the Presidency in the summer of 1923, he seemed to personify the desire of the American people for greater circumspection in the White House. Everything about him was certainly circumspect. Son of a Vermont farmer and storekeeper, he even had the good fortune of being born on Independence Day in 1872. While practicing law in Northampton, Massachusetts, after his graduation from staid Amherst College, he entered politics via membership in the city council. Thereafter he was almost continually in office—rising from city solicitor to clerk of the courts, mayor, state senator, lieutenant governor, and governor. It was not, however, until he became a local hero and a national figure as a result of his handling of the Boston police strike of 1919 that he attracted wide prominence and, in consequence, the Republican Vice Presidential nomination in 1920.

Coolidge's birthplace in Plymouth, Vermont.

Among the best stories about Coolidge's taciturnity are these related by Quincy Howe: When asked why he dined out so much as Vice President, Coolidge remarked, "Got to eat somewhere." At a dinner party his partner confided that a friend had bet her ten dollars she could not make him say three words. "You lose," Coolidge quietly replied. Upon being asked what the minister said about sin in his Sunday sermon, he responded, "He was against it." When a messenger from the Treasury Department handed him his first pay check as President, he mumbled "Call again."

Coolidge the Vermont farmer wearing cowhide boots, a smock, and a frugal smile.

Genial Governor of Massachusetts.

Dapper Amherst College student.

THE COMMONWEALTH OF MASSACHUSETTS
EXECUTIVE DEPARTMENT
STATE HOUSE BOSTON

CALVIN COOLIDGE
GOVERNOR

The main question was not whether the Commissioner or the Governor might not have acted in a different way to preserve order, that was incidental, but whether the Commissioner or the Governor would compromise the authority of the law by permitting that authority to be exercised by a body not chosen by the people for that purpose. They chose to make the authority of the law, exercised only by the chosen representatives of the people, supreme. Any other course would have been revolution.

When Boston's police went on strike in 1919, Coolidge used his authority as Governor of Massachusetts to call out the state militia to protect the city.

In supplementing this statement (left) on the police strike, Coolidge declared, "There is no right to strike against the public safety by anybody, anywhere, at any time." His bold stand in this connection attracted national attention and contributed to his selection as Harding's Vice Presidential running mate.

As Harding's Vice President, Coolidge remained in the background almost unobtrusively.

The Hardings and Coolidges posed together but seldom moved in the same social circles.

391

President and Mrs. Coolidge with their sons Calvin, Jr. and John, in a photo taken in 1924.

The Coolidges in a 1927 photo. Seated next to the President is his father, Col. John Coolidge.

Although lacking ir glamor, President and Mrs. Coolidge brought dignity to the White House.

ay-acting for news photographers at a July Fourth celebration held in Rapid City, South Dakota.

History makers: Elihu Root, Calvin Coolidge and Justice Oliver Wendell Holmes.

Sir Harry and Lady Lauder found the Coolidge humor "delightful and folksy."

Like her husband, Mrs. Calvin Coolidge, the former Grace Goodhue, was a reserved New Englander.

With only a kerosene lamp for light, Coolidge took the Presidential oath of office on August 23, 1923, in the family farmhouse at Plymouth, Vermont. His father (center) administered the oath.

President Coolidge with his Cabinet. Seated, left to right, are Harry S. New, Postmaster General; John W. Weeks, Secretary of War; Charles Evans Hughes, Secretary of State (he was succeeded by Frank Kellogg in 1925); President Coolidge; Andrew W. Mellon, Secretary of the Treasury; Harlan F. Stone, Attorney General; Curtis D. Wilbur, Secretary of the Navy. Standing, left to right, are James J. Davis, Secretary of Labor; Henry C. Wallace, Secretary of Agriculture; Herbert Hoover, Secretary of Commerce; Hubert Work, Secretary of the Interior. Attorney General Stone and Secretary of the Navy Wilbur replaced Harding appointees who were charged with misconduct.

Frank Kellogg (right), Hughes' successor as Secretary of State, and Herbert Hoover (left), Secretary of Commerce, were closer to Coolidge, politically and emotionally, than other members of the Cabinet. As a young lawyer Kellogg fought the paper and oil trusts.

In his first address to Congress on December 6, 1923, Coolidge announced his policies in measured words. Broadcast over the country, his speech stressed economy, integrity.

Washington's elite at a Smithsonian meeting. Left to right in the front row are Treasury Secretary Mellon, Secretary of State Kellogg, President Coolidge, and Chief Justice Taft.

In hauling out the oil-soiled linen of the Teapot Dome scandals of Harding's administration, a Senate Committee found that while the chief culprits were Republicans some Democrats were involved. Hence the above cartoon by John T. McCutcheon. Coolidge appointed Owen J. Roberts, a Republican, and ex-Senator Atlee Pomerene, a Democrat, to prosecute those guilty of misconduct. When Attorney General Harry M. Daugherty (right) became implicated, the President removed him. Former Secretary of the Interior Albert Fall was sent to jail for bribe-taking.

All Indians attained citizenship for the first time by an act of Congress approved by Coolidge in 1924.

Transcontinental air mail service, inaugurated on July 1, 1924, connected east and west overnight.

Only serious competitor for the G.O.P. nomination was Senator Hiram Johnson of California. Chicago banker Charles Gates Dawes, first Director of the Bureau of the Budget, won Vice Presidential nomination.

Unruffled by attacks inspired chiefly by Harding administration scandals, Coolidge ran for a full term in his own right in 1924. His rivals were John W. Davis, chosen on the 103rd ballot of the Democratic convention, and Senator Robert M. LaFollette, candidate of the volatile Progressive Party.

A vote for Coolidge is a vote for the Klan.
A vote for Davis is a vote for the Klan.
A vote for La Follette is a vote **against** the Klan, **against** invisible government, **against** mob rule;

Kool Klammy Kal Koolidge Kant Kondemn the Ku Klux Klan. You Kan Kill the Kruel Ku Klux by Kanning Kunning Kwiet Kal.

Propaganda used against Coolidge by LaFollette supporters who considered him pro-KKK.

Results of the 1924 election by states and counties; the most sanguine hopes were exceeded.

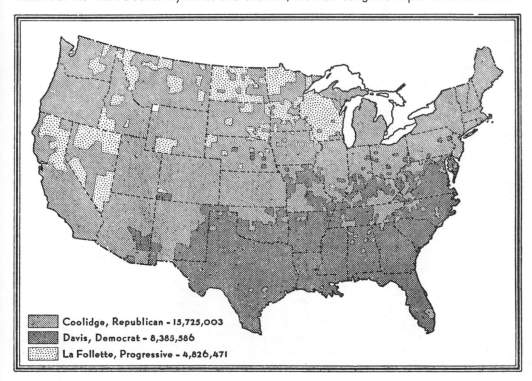

Coolidge, Republican - 15,725,003
Davis, Democrat - 8,385,586
La Follette, Progressive - 4,826,471

Coolidge and Dawes with their wives at the White House on March 4, 1925.

The Coolidges departing for inauguration ceremonies with Sen. Charles Curtis.

President Coolidge and Vice President Dawes in a photo taken a day after 1925 inauguration.

A frugal man in personal as well as national affairs, Coolidge scaled the public debt steadily downward. He approved tax reduction, disapproved the soldiers' bonus.

"Cold and Hot", a cartoon drawn by Seielsted for an editorial in the New York Evening World.

"Economy," Coolidge once said, "is idealism in its most practical form." Sparing even of words, his taciturnity was almost spectacular. "There is no precedent the world over for such a record," relates journalist Henry L. Stoddard. "Never before nor anywhere has silence fashioned a figure that so deeply interested a whole nation, or that caught the favor of so many people. When finally he spoke he was listened to as a master of words that people readily understood — a voice from the fireside or plain, neighborly ways of life. Here was a man, they said, as solid in thought as the marble of his native state, to whom home on a farm or in a two-family house was more familiar than in a mansion, who was bred to ideals other than the hasty pursuit of wealth or the emptiness of society, who lived in their own manner and who was one of them."

An outspoken critic of long-winded deliberations, Vice President Dawes bluntly urged revision of Senatorial procedures so a majority vote could apply closure to debates.

Brusque and picturesque in both speech and manner, "Hell and Maria" Dawes entered the political arena in the 1890's as a key figure in the nomination of William McKinley. In the course of his many-sided career he attained prominence as a leading Chicago lawyer and banker, as Comptroller of the Currency, as a Brigadier General during World War I, as the first Director of the U.S. Budget, as the author of the "Dawes Plan" for post-war German finances, as Ambassador to Great Britain, and, in 1932, as the organizer of the Reconstruction Finance Corporation. The Nobel Peace Prize was awarded to him in 1925. "Hell and Maria" was a favorite figure of speech he used when indignant.

Uncle Sam: "There are no doors in this one"— a cartoon inspired by Dawes' plan for Germany.

Hot-tempered John L. Lewis and Secretary of Labor Davis were on distinctly cordial talking terms. The Shepherd-Towner Act expanded the operations of the Labor Department.

Factory conditions of this sort were fast disappearing. Collective bargaining was sponsored by the government for the first time through the United States Board of Mediation in 1926.

Washington paid tumultuous tribute to audacious Charles A. Lindbergh upon his return from his non-stop flight from New York to Paris in 1927. In bestowing a colonelcy on the intrepid flyer, Coolidge called attention to the progress made by American aviation with government aid since 1921.

Signing of the Kellogg-Briand Treaty (Pact of Paris) was a major diplomatic event of 1928; 62 nations agreed to "condemn recourse to war for the solution of international problems."

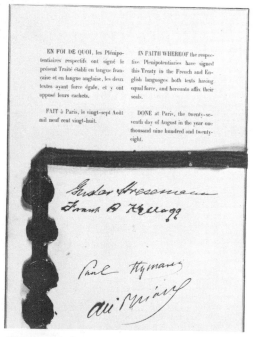

Signers of the pact pledged themselves to respect the territorial integrity of China.

Secretary of State Kellogg promoted the treaty with help of French Premier Aristide Briand.

Marked by almost uninterrupted prosperity, Coolidge's administration saw—and facilitated—an extraordinary rise in the standard of living, a substantial increase in wages, greater business profits, and, some economists felt, an unwary optimism about the future of the nation.

Above: A cartoon Clifford Berryman drew for the Evening Star of Washington, D. C.

Right: The initials took on a broader meaning for supporters of Coolidge policies.

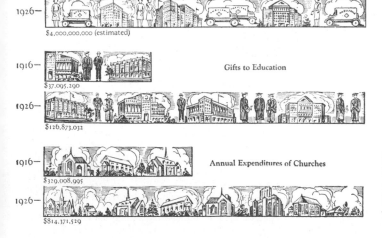

1916—
$1,000,000,000 (estimated)

Value of Hospital Property

1926—
$4,000,000,000 (estimated)

1916—
$37,095,290

Gifts to Education

1926—
$126,873,032

1916—
$329,008,995

Annual Expenditures of Churches

1926—
$814,371,529

Left: As this pictorial chart indicates, material prosperity made possible gigantic strides in the fields of medical service, education, and religion.

In this characteristically terse note Coolidge let it be known that he had decided against seeking nomination for another term in the White House

I do not choose to run for President in nineteen twenty eight

"Crisis in Washington: Mr. Coolidge refuses point blank to vacate the White House until his other rubber is found." This cartoon by Gluyas Williams amused the readers of Life in the spring of 1928.

410

The personal success story of Herbert Hoover surely surpasses that of Horatio Alger's heroes. The son of an Iowa blacksmith of Quaker persuasion, he was orphaned at the age of ten, reared by farming relatives, and educated largely through his own efforts. After graduating from Stanford University, he embarked upon an engineering career, quickly proving his mettle as a mining prospector, promoter, and executive. At 25 he became the head of China's Department of Mines. Positions of increasing importance took him to Australia, Africa, and Europe. By 1914 he had already amassed several million dollars through his far-flung enterprises. When the first World War broke out he sprang into prominence as the director of aid for the thousands of Americans stranded in Europe; subsequently he directed relief for starving millions in the war-devastated countries. Upon American entry into the war, President Wilson appointed him United States Food Administrator. In 1921 he began a new career when President Harding selected him Secretary of Commerce—a post he continued to hold until his nomination for President in 1928. As the head of the Department of Commerce, he assumed dynamic leadership in the development of American business and the promotion of trade with other countries. "One may say," Mark Sullivan observed, "that Hoover regarded our entire business structure as a single factory, conceiving himself, as it were, consulting engineer for the whole enterprise. Having this conception, Hoover set about applying to the whole business structure of the United States principles similar to those which Henry Ford successfully appiled to the manufacture of automobiles."

Herbert Hoover's birthplace at West Branch, Iowa—a painting by fellow-Iowan Grant Wood.

China's mining expert in 1899.

U.S. Food Administrator in 1919.

Belgian interlude (left to right): Crown Prince Leopold, Hoover, Queen Elizabeth, and King Albert. Following his supervision of aid to Americans stranded in Europe upon the outbreak of World War I, Hoover was put in charge of relief work in devastated Belgium.

Vacation idyll: Hoover with a National Park official in the 1920's. While Secretary of Commerce, he promoted conservation of fisheries.

Scholarly Mrs. Herbert Hoover helped her husband translate into English Agricola's mediaeval Latin classic "De Re Metallica".

The Coolidges visiting with the Hoovers during 1928.

Commerce Secretary Hoover and Secretary of Labor James Davis.

He had more on the ball than onlookers realized when he made this pitch.

"Futuristic Music," a cartoon by Thomas in the Detroit News. As Secretary of Commerce during the Harding and Coolidge administrations, Hoover seemed to be the busiest person in Washington, D. C.

"The Traffic Problem in Washington" by J. N. Ding.

Hoover built the Department of Commerce into a dynamic agency, giving particular attention to the expansion of American trade at home and abroad and the development of the fast burgeoning radio and aviation industries. He initiated the St. Lawrence waterway and was considered chiefly responsible for the establishment of the Federal Radio Commission, predecessor of the present Federal Communications Commission.

Coolidge's blessing made Hoover's nominatoin for President almost certain.

"The Bandwagon Rush", a cartoon in Washington's Evening Star.

As had been generally anticipated, Hoover won the party's nomination in 1928 on the first ballot and by an overwhelming majority. Senator Charles Curtis was chosen his running mate.

"The Choice of Weapons", a cartoon in the Detroit News.

The Chicago Daily News struck a responsive chord when it printed this piece of doggerel:

"Who kept the Belgians'
    black bread buttered?
Who fed the world when
    millions muttered?
Who knows the needs of
    every nation?
Who keeps the keys of
    conservation?
Who fills the bins when
    mines aren't earning?
Who keeps the home fires
    banked and burning?
Who'll never win Presiden-
    tial position,
For he isn't a practical
    politician?
Hoover—that's all!"

"The Show-Down", a cartoon by J. N. Ding in the New York Herald Tribune. To the surprise of supporters of Alfred E. Smith, Hoover received a plurality of 103,481 votes in New York State.

As a co-owner of several ranches in California's San Joaquin Valley, Hoover helped transform barren lands into fertile fields which produced ten harvests a year in triple crops with grain, fruit, and cotton following one another in rotation. Such modern farm machinery as motor plows, harvesters, reapers, stalk cutters, mechanical sprayers, and electric refrigerators were employed, at Hoover's urging, so effectively that the ranch values tripled in a few years. Campaign propaganda also reminded the nation of the progress made by American agriculture when Hoover served as U.S. Food Administrator during the trying days of World War I.

"Truly Rural", a cartoon by Marcus in the New York Times.

419

A Chicken *for* Every Pot

THE Republican Party isn't a *"Poor Man's Party:"* Republican prosperity has erased that degrading phrase from our political vocabulary.

The Republican Party is *equality's* party—*opportunity's* party—*democracy's* party, the party of *national* development, not *sectional* interests—the *impartial* servant of every State and condition in the Union.

Under higher tariff and lower taxation, America has stabilized output, employment and dividend rates.

Republican efficiency has filled the workingman's dinner pail—and his gasoline tank *besides*—made telephone, radio and sanitary plumbing *standard* household equipment. And placed the whole nation in the *silk stocking class*.

During eight years of Republican management, we have built more and better homes, erected more skyscrapers, passed more benefactory laws, and more laws to regulate and purify immigration, inaugurated more conservation measures, more measures to standardize and increase production, expand export markets, and reduce industrial and human junk piles, than in any previous quarter century.

Republican prosperity is written on *fuller* wage envelops, written in factory chimney smoke, written on the walls of new construction, written in savings bank books, written in mercantile balances, and written in the peak value of stocks and bonds.

Republican prosperity has *reduced* hours and *increased* earning capacity, silenced *discontent*, put the proverbial "chicken in every pot." And a car in every backyard, to boot.

It has *raised* living standards and *lowered* living costs.

It has restored financial confidence and enthusiasm, changed *credit* from a *rich* man's privilege to a *common* utility, *generalized* the use of time-saving devices and released women from the thrall of *domestic drudgery*.

It has provided every county in the country with its concrete road and knitted the highways of the nation into a *unified* traffic system.

Thanks to Republican administration, farmer, dairyman and merchant can make deliveries in *less* time and at *less* expense, can borrow *cheap* money to re-fund exorbitant mortgages, and stock their pastures, ranges and shelves.

Democratic management *impoverished* and *demoralized* the *railroads*, led packing plants and tire factories into *receivership*, squandered billions on *impractical* programs.

Democratic mal-administration issued *further* billions on mere "scraps of paper," then encouraged foreign debtors to believe that their loans would never be called, and bequeathed to the Republican Party the job of *mopping up the mess*.

Republican administration has *restored* to the railroads solvency, efficiency and par securities.

It has brought the rubber trades through panic and chaos, brought down the prices of crude rubber by smashing *monopolistic rings*, put the tanner's books in the *black* and secured from the European powers formal acknowledgment of their obligations.

The Republican Party rests its case on a record of stewardship and performance.

Its Presidential and Congressional candidates stand for election on a platform of sound practice, Federal vigilance, high tariff, Constitutional integrity, the conservation of natural resources, *honest* and *constructive* measures for agricultural relief, sincere enforcement of the laws, and the right of *all* citizens, regardless of *faith* or *origin*, to share the benefits of opportunity and justice.

Wages, dividends, progress and prosperity say,

"Vote *for* Hoover"

Contributed by a Friend of Mr. Hoover

Advertisement.

An anonymous supporter paid for this full-page newspaper advertisement during the campaign.

"Neck and Neck at the Quarter Pole"—a cartoon J. N. Ding drew for publication on election day. "It was obvious from the beginning of the campaign," Herbert Hoover relates in his memoirs, "that I should win if we made no mistakes. General prosperity was on my side . . . During the campaign Governor Smith said no word and engaged in no action that did not comport with the highest levels. I paid a natural tribute to him when speaking in New York during the campaign and he did so to me when speaking in California. In after years, when I was often associated with him in public matters, we mutually agreed that we had one deep satisfaction from the battle. No word had been spoken or misrepresentation made by either of us."

The first Republican candidate since Reconstruction days to carry a substantial part of the South, Hoover received majorities in nine states below the Mason-Dixon line and was swept into office by an overwhelming popular vote of 21,500,000 as compared with 15,005,000 for Alfred E. Smith. However, he lost Massachusetts and Rhode Island, which, with one exception, had gone Republican at every Presidential election since 1860. Public interest was so intense that approximately six million more votes were cast in 1928 than in 1924.

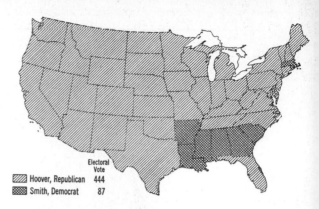

Electoral
Vote
Hoover, Republican   444
Smith, Democrat   87

An extraordinary landslide victory placed Herbert Hoover in the White House. He carried forty states.

Improved inter-American relations were fostered by the President-elect during a good-will cruise to South America prior to his inauguration. Responding to criticism of "dollar diplomacy" under Harding and Coolidge, he discontinued intervention in Latin American affairs and withdrew U.S. occupation troops.

"Another Link", a drawing by Charles Kuhn in the Indianapolis News.

Cold rain drops fell on Hoover's bare head as he repeated aloud the oath of office sonorously quoted to him by Chief Justice Taft. A drenched crowd saw his lips touch the verse from the Book of Proverbs he had chosen as his text for the occasion: "Where there is no vision, the people perish; but he that keepeth the law, happy is he." Although fellow Quakers expected the new President to express "affirmation" of his responsibilities under the Constitution, he took the regular oath despite the traditional objection of his co-religionists to "swearing" of any type.

423

Above: The secretarial staff of the new Vice President. Note the chic fashions of the day.

Vice President Charles Curtis, seen above with Representative Mondell, served in Congress thirty-three years. The first American of Indian blood to attain prominence in national affairs, Curtis was also the first Vice President to be born west of the Mississippi River. His mother was a quarter-blood member of the Kaw tribe in Kansas.

A photograph of President Hoover with Hubert Work at his right and Claudius H. Huston at his left. The latter replaced Work as Chairman of the Republican National Committee.

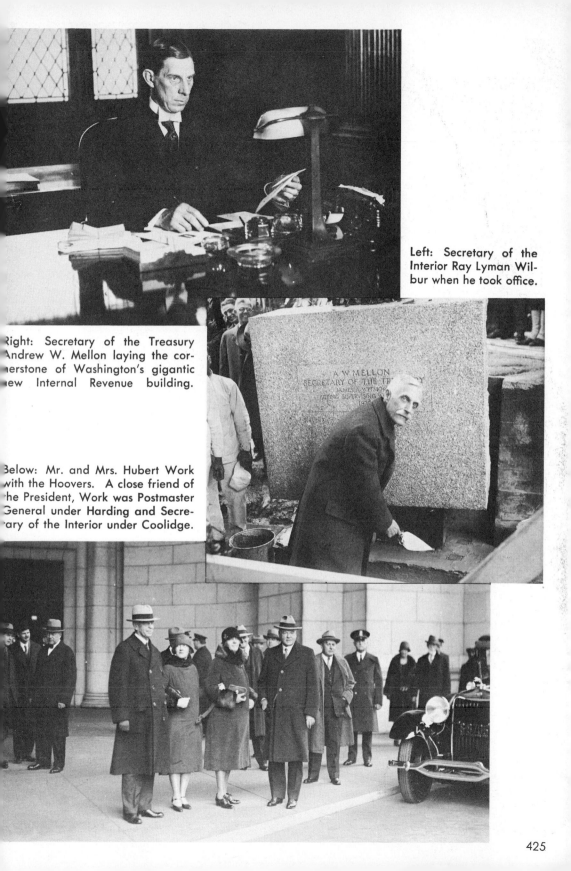

Left: Secretary of the Interior Ray Lyman Wilbur when he took office.

Right: Secretary of the Treasury Andrew W. Mellon laying the cornerstone of Washington's gigantic new Internal Revenue building.

Below: Mr. and Mrs. Hubert Work with the Hoovers. A close friend of the President, Work was Postmaster General under Harding and Secretary of the Interior under Coolidge.

425

Hoover with his cabinet. Left to right in the front row: Walter F. Brown, Postmaster General; James W. Good, Secretary of War; Frank B. Kellogg, Secretary of State; Andrew Mellon, Secretary of the Treasury; William D. Mitchell, Attorney General. Back row: James J. Davis, Secretary of Labor; Robert P. Lamont, Secretary of Commerce; Arthur M. Hyde, Secretary of Agriculture; Vice President Charles Curtis; Ray Lyman Wilbur, Secretary of the Interior; and Charles Francis Adams, Secretary of the Navy.

Henry L. Stimson, Kellogg's successor as Secretary of State, is seen signing the oath of office as Kellogg and Chief Justice Taft look on. Stimson also served in Taft's cabinet.

The first gigantic multiple-purpose dam, the Hoover Dam was blueprinted in 1929 with the President's engineering advice. It harnesses the Colorado River where the latter forms the boundary between Arizona and Nevada. Its huge reservoir impounds flood waters for use in irrigation, silt control, the generation of hydro-electric energy, and the improvement of navigation. Other great reclamation projects were soon to follow.

Members of the National Law Enforcement Commission appointed in 1929 made an exhaustive investigation which helped local and national authorities combat crime.

Jailed through the efforts of the Justice Department, gangster Al Capone reached the end of his bullet-ridden career. Falsification of income tax returns led to his conviction.

"Gulliver and the Lilliputians" expresses what many newspapers felt. While chiefly opposed by Democratic Congressmen, Hoover was also handicapped by criticism from Republican legislators.

In establishing the Federal Farm Board (seen above with Hoover) in 1929, Congress initially authorized it to spend $500 million for miscellaneous agricultural relief purposes.

NATION-WIDE FEVER OF STOCK SPECULATION

Eager Buying Has Reached All Classes of People Throughout the Country and Has Set New Records In Many Directions—Effects of Struggle to Grasp Profits in Trading in Securities Are Evident

A forewarning of the shape of things to come. The N. Y. Times noted with alarm the tendency of the public to be easily influenced by unreliable rumors about stocks.

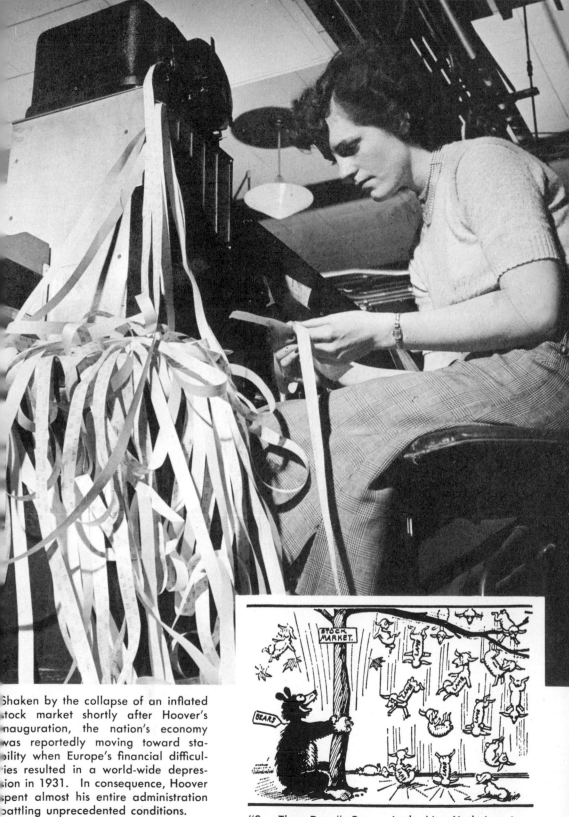

Shaken by the collapse of an inflated stock market shortly after Hoover's inauguration, the nation's economy was reportedly moving toward stability when Europe's financial difficulties resulted in a world-wide depression in 1931. In consequence, Hoover spent almost his entire administration battling unprecedented conditions.

"See Them Drop"—Powers in the New York American.

The following steps were taken during Hoover's administration to accomplish economic recovery: (1) The Federal Farm Board was authorized to furnish agricultural relief. (2) The Employment Stabilization Act was passed to minimize unemployment. (3) A moratorium on World War I debts was declared. (4) International short-term credits were extended under a "stand-still agreement". (5) The National Credit Association was organized under Federal auspices to assist banking institutions in financial difficulties. (6) The Reconstruction Finance Corporation was established to make loans to business firms and to finance state-sponsored relief and public work projects. (7) Agricultural credit banks were created with authority to make $1,000,000,000 available for farm production and livestock purposes. (8) The Federal Land Banks were strengthened with $1,000,000,000 for farm mortgages. (9) Twelve Home Loan Banks were established to provide $1,000,000,000 to save homes and farms from foreclosure. (10) The Federal Reserve Board was authorized to counteract inflation by expanding credit to business and banks. (11) Thousands of failures were prevented through a revision of the bankruptcy laws. "Apart from the Roosevelt measures of reform," observed Walter Lippmann in 1935, "all the main features of the Roosevelt program were anticipated by Mr. Hoover."

Recalled to Washington to head up the newly formed Reconstruction Finance Corporation, former Vice President Charles G. Dawes served as close adviser to Hoover.

Labor leaders calling upon the President were urged to prevent strikes and cooperate in spreading employment through shortened work days. The rights of trade unions were strengthened by the passage in 1932 of the Norris-LaGuardia Act outlawing "Yellow Dog" contracts and limiting the use of injunctions in labor disputes. Federal employment offices were increased and the Bacon-Davis Act provided for payment of prevailing wages to persons on government projects. A. F. of L. President William Green is in center of front row.

HOOVER ASKS $150,000,000 TO AID IDLE; WARNS OF DEFICIT AND END OF TAX CUT; HIS CONTROL OF WORKS FUND OPPOSED

OPPOSE HOOVER METHODS

Democrats and Some Republicans Disagree With His Relief Program.

PARTY REGULARS PRAISE IT

Most of Leaders Are for Putting the Proposals Into Force Without Delay.

WALL STREET IS PLEASED

Holds Ideas for Business Sound —Press Hails Avoidance of Controversial Matters.

Bills Laid Before Congress on Employment Relief And to Deal With Country's Economic Recovery

Special to The New York Times.

WASHINGTON, Dec. 2.—Measures on employment relief and economic recovery introduced in the Senate and House today included the following:

By Senator Glenn—A resolution to carry out President Hoover's recommendation for an emergency fund of $150,000,000 to accelerate public works.

By Senators Robinson of Arkansas, McNary and Caraway—Resolutions to provide $60,000,000 to aid drought-stricken farmers.

By Senator Blaine—Bill for creating a Federal industrial commission to study the stabilization of employment.

By Senator Capper—Resolution to distribute 40,000,000 bushels of the Farm Board's wheat surplus to relief organizations for food.

By Senator Brookhart—Bill increasing appropriations for public roads from $125,000,00 to $500,000,000 for two years.

By Senator Keyes and Representative Elliott—Twin bills to expedite work on Federal buildings.

By Senator Reed—Bill to suspend immigration for two years from all countries on this hemisphere and from Europe.

By Representative Cable—Bill to exclude all immigration of laborers until the Secretary of Labor decides they are needed.

By Senator Oddie—Bill to embargo the importation of all products from Soviet Russia.

By Representative Huddleston—Bill to appropriate $50,000,000 to be used by the President as a "destitution fund."

MESSAGE READ TO CONGRESS

President Asks Speed on Bills to Create Work in Next Six Months.

URGES PUBLIC COOPERATION

He Advocates Federal Loans to Farmers—Hits at Speculation as a Cause of Depression.

TREASURY LOSS $180,000,000

Action on Muscle Shoals and Inquiry for Changing Anti-Trust Law Recommended.

The New York Times coverage of President Hoover's message to Congress on December 2, 1930.

"Every Little Bit Helps" (left) and "Rally 'Round the Flag" (right) epitomized support by the press.

433

From the steps of the Ripon, Wisconsin, schoolhouse in which the G.O.P. was born, Secretary of War Patrick J. Hurley opened Hoover's 1932 reelection campaign opposing Franklin D. Roosevelt.

"Speaking of Nerve-Wracking Noises", a cartoon by Clifford Berryman in Washington's Evening Star. Democratic strategy was to place the blame for the depression on the Republican doorstep. Policies under Harding and Coolidge were played up as major contributions to difficult times.

| WHAT TO DO IN A STORM | IN THE NAME OF COMMON SENSE, WHY CHANGE? |

Cartoons distributed by the Republican National Committee during the 1932 campaign. The item on the left, drawn by J. N. Ding, originally appeared in the New York Herald Tribune.

A popular post-card propaganda piece. Following the election of Franklin D. Roosevelt, Hoover upset precedent by inviting him to the White House to confer regarding pending problems.

EXPANSION OF THE UNITED STATES

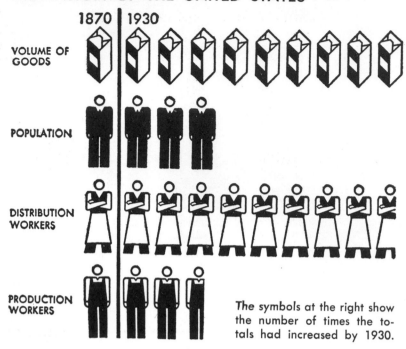

The symbols at the right show the number of times the totals had increased by 1930.

Almost continuously in power from 1860 to 1932—excepting only the administrations of Cleveland and Wilson—the Republican Party could claim (and did) immense credit for the extraordinary progress of the nation during this period. If it was loathe to accept responsibility for the things that went awry, the Democrats surely made the most of this.

INCREASE OF HIGHWAYS AND VEHICLES

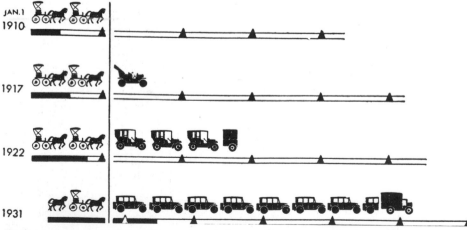

Each pictograph on the right represents three million motor vehicles. Spaces between the vertical markers symbolize 500,000 miles of road; surfaced portions are dark.

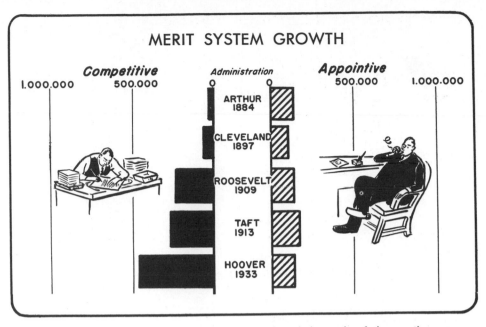

MERIT SYSTEM GROWTH

Competitive

1.000.000   500.000

Administration

Appointive

500.000   1.000.000

ARTHUR 1884

CLEVELAND 1897

ROOSEVELT 1909

TAFT 1913

HOOVER 1933

Slowly but surely the federal civil service replaced the evils of the spoils system.

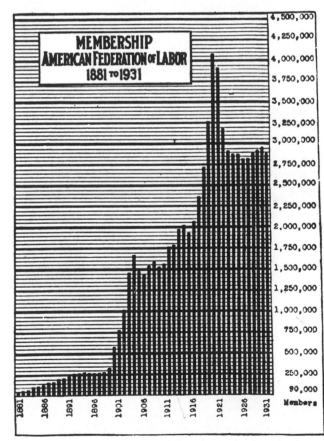

MEMBERSHIP AMERICAN FEDERATION OF LABOR 1881 TO 1931

Trade unionism made gigantic strides as the lot of the worker improved under Republican leadership.

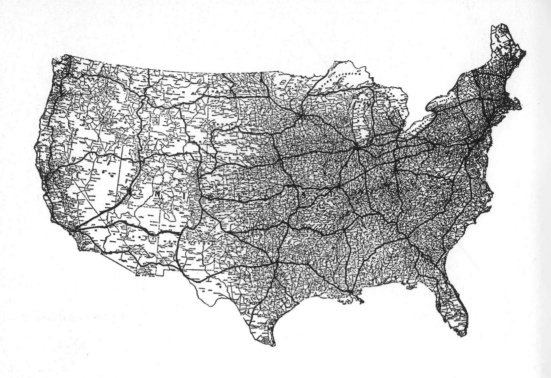

Characteristic of the nation's material growth was the tremendous expansion of telephone service (depicted above) and railroad lines (shown below).

Diametrically the opposite of his Democratic rival, Franklin D. Roosevelt, in personality, character, and political philosophy, Alfred Mossman Landon has been aptly called "the Kansas Coolidge". Although verbose by comparison with the tight-lipped New Englander, he had much in common with him. Both had a deeply rooted sense of frugality (Landon struck a tender chord with his campaign credo "I believe a man can be a liberal without being a spendthrift"), both lived simply and unostentatiously, both spent most of their lives in local rather than national politics, both rose to be governors of their states without the benefit of high-powered organization support, and both had strict moral codes. But they were distinctly different men in some basic respects.

The Landon family posing for a photograph in the living room of their Topeka home.

Halfback Alf Landon (top row, left) is seen here with classmates at Marietta Academy.

A photo of the 1936 convention delegates.

Born in the parsonage of his grandfather, a Methodist minister, Landon had strong streaks of preacher, promoter, and politician from his boyhood days. After graduating from law school without generating any overwhelming desire to be a lawyer, he became a bank clerk by day and an oil prospector by night. He got his first taste of politics at the Bull Moose convention of 1912. In subsequent years he became active in Kansas politics and rose to such popularity that he was the sole G.O.P. gubernatorial candidate elected west of the Mississippi in 1932; two years later he was the only Republican Governor in the entire country to be reelected. By the spring of 1936 his nomination for President was all but taken for granted by party leaders. Although relatively unknown to the public at large, he had the advantage of having few enemies or critics. "I think Landon is marvelous," said William Randolph Hearst. Writing for the usually anti-Republican "Nation", commentator Raymond Gram Swing declared in one of his articles, "Landon is a gifted executive who is not much less progressive in philosophy than Franklin D. Roosevelt."

The comparison of Abe and Alf seemed strained to journalist Water Lippmann.

IT'S LIKE THAT OUT IN KANSAS

If you ask where, in our troubled land,
There's a spot by bracing breezes fanned;
Kissed by the sunshine, bedewed by night,
Where God's in His Heaven and right is right;
Where Nature sheds her blandest smile
As rippling fields spread mile on mile;
Where men and women of sterling worth
Are honored still as the salt of the earth;
 —The answer's out in Kansas.

Where, in the annals of rugged men,
Is a race that can rise and smile again
When tragic years of drought drag by
And billows of dust pile mountain high;
That yields no ground, that signs no truce
Be all the devils of hell turned loose;
Dreams no weak dreams of utopian bliss
Since freedom was bought at a price like this:
 —No place but out in Kansas.

Kansas—child of the wide free West!
Kansas—close to the nation's breast;
Hearing that great heart's troubled beat
Sends far her call—"Men don't retreat!
Hold to your freedom! Fling out that flag
From staff and steeple, mast and crag,
And when the dust and storms are past
Heaven will smile on our land at last!"
 —They know that out in Kansas.

Bursting acres rich with grain,
Touched by the magic gift of rain;
Meadows green where the dew distills;
The cattle on ten thousand hills;
Food for all in this favored spot,
Food for a million men forgot;
Friend to the stranger within her gates;
Love for all her sister states.
 —It's like that out in Kansas.

When power-mad men with fell design
Weave schemes that subtly undermine
The fair high precepts of our realm;
With crafty promise, steal the helm;
Bestrew the land with stupid wrongs
That bind free men with alien thongs,
At these — does Kansas cringe in fear?
NO! SHE RIDES WITH PAUL REVERE!
 —It's a habit out in Kansas.

If, in a time of deep concern,
A sore pressed people gravely turn
Seeking a man with calm clear mind,
Rich in the virtues of mankind;
Who sets not man against his brother
But urges justice one to the other,
Who, living close to the friendly sod
Yet looks away to the stars and God,
 —The stars that shine on Kansas.

If a man they want for the crucial hour
Who courts no Caesar's dream of power;
Proud of the glories of his state
And the precepts that made his nation great;
True to the liberties that men love best;
Son of the virile abounding West,
Full-charged with zeal to speed the day
Of a nation rejoicing on its way,
 —They'll find him out in Kansas!

By Burton H. Pugh, Topeka, Kansas
Copyrighted 1936
Reprinted by special permission

ALFRED PANEPINTO

Dedicated to Governor Landon, this poem by Burton H. Pugh was widely circulated.

"A Son of the People" versus "A Scion of Wealth", a poster by Alfred Panepinto.

He's One of Us!

ALL AMERICA SWINGS TO LANDON

The first page of an illustrated pamphlet distributed by the Republican National Committee.

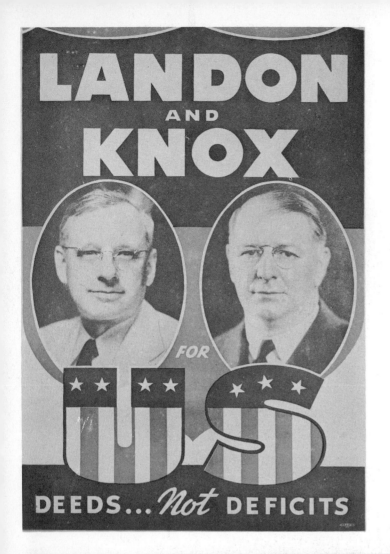

Expenditures under the Ne
Deal were scored heavily
posters such as one on left.
believe," Landon averred,
man can be a liberal witho
being a spendthrift."

Among those who supported t
Landon-Knox ticket were prom
nent ex-Democrats and offic
holders during Democratic a
ministrations: Alfred E. Smit
Presidential nominee of 192
James A. Reed, former Senat
from Missouri; "Alfalfa Bi
Murray, onetime Governor
Oklahoma; Lewis Douglas, D
rector of the Budget during t
early days of the New Dea
Bainbridge Colby, Secretary
State under Wilson; and Josep
M. Ely, ex-Governor of Mas

Thousands of such billboards left no doubt as to Republican opinion of the New Deal

ominated for Vice President by cclamation, Colonel Frank Knox ppealed to progressive elements in the party. After serving with the Rough Riders during he war with Spain, he supported Theodore Roosevelt during he campaigns of 1900, 1904, nd 1908. Although he strayed om the party fold during the ull Moose days, President Taft ppointed him to the Board of dian Commissioners. When the .S. entered World War I, he nlisted and rose quickly to the ank of Lieutenant Colonel. In ubsequent years he became, uccessively, editor of the Boston merican, General Manager of he Hearst papers, and publisher of the Chicago Daily News.

As Secretary of the Navy during World War II, Knox rendered distinguished service   447

ILLINOIS REPUBLICAN STATE CENTRAL COMMITTEE
PERRY B. McCULLOUGH CHAIRMAN

LINCOLN

WASHINGTON

G.O.P. MARCH

WORDS AND MUSIC BY
GUST SAFSTROM

For President

DeMOTTE MUSIC CO.
835 EAST 75th STREET
· CHICAGO ·
ILLINOIS
TELEPHONE - VINCENNES 9663

SOLD TO HELP FINANCE THE 1936 CAMPAIGN
PRICE 10 CENTS

For Vice-President

Gov. ALF LANDON

Col. FRANK KNOX

448 Campaign spirits as well as funds were raised with the help of this song by Gust Safstrom.

Countless copies of this derisive propaganda item were distributed by Frank C. Hughes of Maine.

...inning in the manner of the Declaration of Independence, the Republican platform of 1936 proclaimed: "For ...ee long years the New Deal administration has dis...ored American traditions and flagrantly betrayed the ...dges upon which the Democratic Party sought and re...ved public support." By way of substantiation it charged ...t Franklin D. Roosevelt had usurped the powers of ...ngress, that the integrity of the Supreme Court had been ...unted, that "the rights and liberties of American citizens" ...d been violated, and that free enterprise had been dis...ced by "regulated monopoly". On the positive side the ...tform promised maintenance of "the American system of ...stitutional and local self-government", preservation of ...ditional free enterprise, "encouragement instead of hin...nce to legitimate business", and replacement of "uncon...led spending" with a "balanced budget". On foreign ...icy the platform took the position that "America shall ... become a member of the League of Nations". At ...ht is a Newark Evening News cartoon by Lute Pease.

Another type of promotional currency, this certificate was used in soliciting campaign funds.

"Pointing Straight to Washington", a cartoon in the Chicago Tribune.

"To the Rescue", a cartoon by Alfred Panepinto in the Republican Challenge of September 1936.

The G.O.P. serenade was almost drowned out by an economic upswing for which Democratic New Dealers claimed chief credit.

The Republican ticket lost the electoral votes of all but two states—Vermont and Maine. "Think of Spain, vote like Maine" was a party slogan which went unheeded.

The Kansas sunflower bloomed all too briefly. Even on a county basis, as shown in map below, the election results left much to be desired.

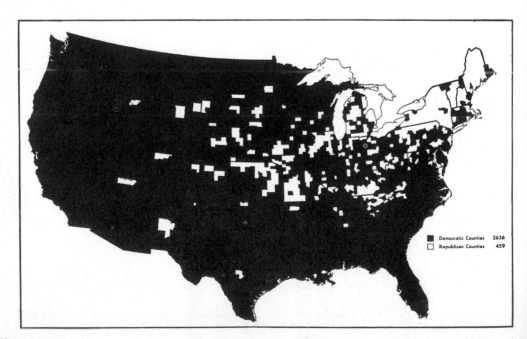

■ Democratic Counties   2636
□ Republican Counties   459

A unique phenomenon in American politics, Wendell Lewis Willkie brought to the campaign o
1940 a dynamic personality, boundless energy, and a one-man social force. Not since Theodore
Roosevelt had there been anyone quite like him; beside him such figures as Coolidge, Hoover, and
Landon seemed pallid. Without any political experience whatsoever he shot into the Presidentia
race while old-timers looked on with amazement. The influences which shaped his life and char
acter explain the man only in part. His liberalism stemmed from his grandfather, who fled Ger
many after the abortive revolution of 1848 against Prussian autocracy. His warm heart and keer
mind were nourished in a family atmosphere of emotional frankness and intellectual stimulation
His father, an immigrant, rose to circuit judge in Indiana; his mother, a teacher in her youth, be
came the state's first woman attorney. Raised in the best Hoosier tradition, Wendell was a brigh
but restless boy. Misfortune proved a steadying influence; when his father lost heavily in rea
estate ventures, the lad hired himself out as a farm hand and earned enough to pay part of hi
expenses at the University of Indiana. A campus "barbarian", he rebelled against fraternities
challenged the Bible, and preached sophomoric socialism. When the novelty of non-conformism
wore off he switched to Jeffersonian democracy and settled down to preparation for the bar

oon graduating from law school Wendell Willkie courted and married vivacious Edith Wilk, a pert rarian, and sailed for France with the A.E.F. When he returned he set up law practice in Akron, hio, launched a drive against the KKK, and became closely associated with the Commonwealth and outhern Corporation. As top officer of the latter enterprise—he became its president when he was 2—he not only led one of the nation's largest public utility systems in the development of the ectric power age, but, what turned out to be more significant, he spearheaded one of the most pirited battles against the New Deal. In speeches, in articles, and in deeds he waged a relentless ar on F.D.R. and all his works. "No duty has ever come to me in my life," he explained, "even at in the service of my country, which has so appealed to my sense of social obligation, patriotism, nd love of mankind as this, my obligation to say and do what I can for the preservation of public tilities privately owned." First to sense his political potentialities, Fortune magazine remarked: Wendell Willkie is the Mississippi Yankee, the clever bumpkin, the homespun, rail-splitting, cracker-arrel simplifier of national issues." Overnight Willkie-for-President clubs began springing up roughout the country. When the Republican convention opened in June 1940 he encountered rong opposition because he had been a registered Democrat most of his life (not until 1938 did e enter the G.O.P. fold with the explanation that "perhaps the Democratic Party left me"), et he snatched the Presidential nomination from under the noses of Vandenberg, Dewey and Taft.

eleven Wendell appeared in this photograph anding at left) with his brothers and father.

A Lieutenant in the artillery during World War I; hostilities ended while he was in France.

Fellow students at Indiana University were fascinated by his oratory and crusading spirit.

As spokesman for the drive against public ownership of utilities, Willkie received much publicity.

On "Information Please", Willkie outshone encyclopaedic John Kieran (left) and wit F. P. Adams.

Four brothers (left to right): Robert, Edward, Wendell and Fred Willkie in a 1940 photograph.

WENDELL L. WILLKIE

The Story of
A Country Boy
Who Made Good
and Why
THE REPUBLICAN
CONVENTION
Nominated him for
PRESIDENT
OF THE
UNITED STATES.

The Story begins in Elwood, Indiana, February, 18, 1892

In what year
was the Dalton
Gang's raid?
Who was the
greatest base-
ball pitcher?

Who discovered
Africa?

IMPORTANT
COFFEYVILLE
HISTORY

COPR. 1940 - ALBER

(3)
As driver of a delivery wagon
young Willkie learned how to hitch
up a horse and about horse power
which afterward stood him in good
stead when he began putting thousands of horse power together

(1)
Two Elwood neighbors were passing Herman Willkie's home. One
of them said,—"Herm's got a new
kid. He sure has got a husky pair
of lungs. Should be able to make
himself heard later on,—eh?"

(2)
This youngster grew into a healthy
rough and tumble boy,—inventor
and leader in pranks. He never
sought trouble, but if trouble
overtook him he did not let it bluff him

BAKERY

(6)
Ambitiou
get ahead
up the stu
law in In
University
walked of
honors an
tered his
er's law of
On the day
United St
declared
volunteere
a private.
back a Cap

The rise of Wendell Willkie from farm boy to Presidential candidate of the Republican Party.

Husked corn in Iowa

Worked as short-order cook

at belt | Worked in Texas Oil fields | And always a student

gh jobs, but they made a man of the
ngster who was not afraid to tackle them

(7) After his return from France Wendell Willkie hardly waited to get out of his uniform before he was after a job, for he had married Miss Edith Wilk. He landed a job as attorney for Firestone Tire & Rubber Co.

His remarkable success (8) in winning cases brought him a call from New York to head Commonwealth and Southern. His changes and innovations and his spectacular success which followed, amazed the industry

(5) Young Willkie became teacher of history in the Coffeyville, Kansas High School. He also acted as coach in athletics

(10) The first attempt to "stop Willkie" was when the New Deal High Command sent their toughest terror, Attorney General Robert Jackson, to take him apart at a Town Hall debate in New York. But Bob was the one flattened out and likewise was his presidential balloon

WILLKIE PLAN

(9) Instead of dismissing employees to meet diminishing returns, he hired more people to sell more electrical equipment, which would use more power, reduce the rates and in turn, create more jobs and, incidentally make some profits. It was as simple as that, —and it worked! ∾

IDENTIFICATION CARD
ROBERT H. JACKSON

(11) Willkie awoke next morning to find himself being looked over to head the biggest business in the world, the U.S.A.

(12) It was the New Deal Administration that made Willkie. When they ganged up on him and, at the point of a gun, attempted to take his company which belonged to his thousands of stockholders, he fought,—and won! The Country learned about the man; his courage, ability and accomplishments. John Q. Public jumped to his feet-shouted, "There is our man. Lets go and get him!"

Albert T. Reid

WILLKIE COMPELS T.V.A.'s to pay 32 million dollars more than idolists offered for company

WILLKIE NO QUITTER REFUSES TO BE BULLDOZED

In 1920 he represented the United States as a heavyweight wrestler at the Olympic games.

To the rhythmic chant of his supporters in the galleries, "We — want — Willkie!", his fortunes at the 1940 convention in Philadelphia skyrocketed although he had no orthodox organization behind him, no pledged delegates, and no official manager. From barely 100 votes on the first ballot he rose steadily to victory on the sixth. "Nothing exactly like it ever happened in American politics," reported Newsweek magazine.

The Willkie blitzkrieg in action; even life-long Democrats succumbed.

Brother Edward was a tireless campaign helper in the middle-west.

Old-time politicians looked on with amazement as Willkie barnstormed across the country for fifty-one days and 18,579 miles.

Delivering an address at Mt. Rushmore near Rapid City, South Dakota.

Librarian Edith Wilk changed her name to Mrs. Wendell Willkie in 1918.

WILLKIE   McNARY

Although relatively obscure, Senator Charles L. McNary of Oregon, Willkie's running mate, won strong support for their ticket on the west coast and among farmers. Democratic papers noted that his record in Congress included opposition to some of Willkie's basic ideas. A product of the power-conscious northwest, he had backed TVA and other federal electric projects. Moreover, he had voted for the Securities and Exchange Commission and was inclined toward isolationism. As co-sponsor of the McNary-Haugen Farm Bill in the 1920s he espoused a plan for agricultural relief somewhat similar to that later instituted by the New Deal; this measure called for the establishment of a federal fund for the purchase of surplus farm products at fixed prices. Two versions of the bill were passed by Congress but vetoed by President Coolidge.

Democrats like Alfred E. Smith and Lewis W. Douglas considered Willkie a genuine liberal.

Willkie with Senators Robert Taft and Arthur Vandenberg; their opinions often clashed.

WENDELL WILLKIE *Says:*

"I pledge, if elected President, to enlist the whole-hearted cooperation

DEBTS EXPERIMENTS UNEMPLOYMENT

Clearing the Way

of labor, industry, agriculture and every other group, in the task of overcoming our present economic stagnation, and of wiping out unemployment."

10-14-40

 WENDELL WILLKIE *Says:*

"I deny that Franklin Roosevelt — whatever his intentions — is the defender of democracy. I charge

THIRD TERM HOSTILITY BUREAUCRACY

DEMOCRATIC INSTITUTIONS

A Strain on Democracy

that in America he has strained our democratic institutions to the breaking point. I warn you — and I say this in dead earnest. If, because of some fine speeches about humanity, you return this Administration to office, you will be serving under an American totalitarian government before the long Third Term is finished."

10-15-40

 WENDELL WILLKIE *Says:*

"I stand for the doctrine of protecting American private enterprise

NEW DEAL PROMISES PAY ENVELOPE

Which?

and work. I stand for the protection of every possible social gain, and I stand also for the security of employment against insecurity of employment. If you elect me President of the United States I shall not promise the moon, but I shall promise you jobs in honest work and in honest industry."

10-16-40

 WENDELL WILLKIE *Says:*

"By its sinister rumors the government has created a government-made depression. The economic

HATE ABUSE

Political Brew

suffering of the American people today is not the fault of industry; it is primarily the fault of government.

"The politicians brewed a kind of witch's broth out of a pot of horror and smeared it all over American enterprise.

"Let no one think this campaign of abuse and misrepresentation has come to an end. For one thing, it is too useful in covering up the mistakes of the Administration."

10-17-40

 WENDELL WILLKIE *Says:*

"Let us go forth carrying the same light that we can still see

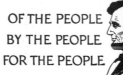

OF THE PEOPLE
BY THE PEOPLE
FOR THE PEOPLE

America's Creed

when we look back to Abraham Lincoln, the greatest of Republicans: the light of government of the people, by the people and for the people. With that light, and with that alone, we shall make our way into the new world. With that light, and with that alone, we shall rebuild America."

10-18-40

 WENDELL WILLKIE *Says:*

"Not even a totalitarian state has more financial powers than those exercised by the present Adminis-

EARNINGS PRICES

New Deal Puppet Show

tration. Such 'rigging' of the markets as the bankers were able to achieve in their heyday in this country was as nothing compared with the financial puppet show put on by the government, in which, by pulling this string and that, the government can lower or raise interest rates, security prices, purchasing power and the value of various commodities."

10-19 or 10-20-40

Six releases of a feature prepared by the Republican National Committee for newspapers.

An added attraction at the Frontier Days celebration in Cheyenne, Wyoming.

"The Flower That Just Growed"—Dowling in the Omaha, Nebraska, World-Herald.

"On His Way"—a cartoon drawn by Robert Messner for the Rochester, N.Y., Times-Union.

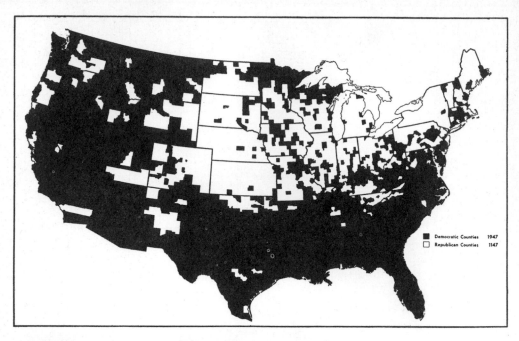

Democratic Counties 1947
Republican Counties 1147

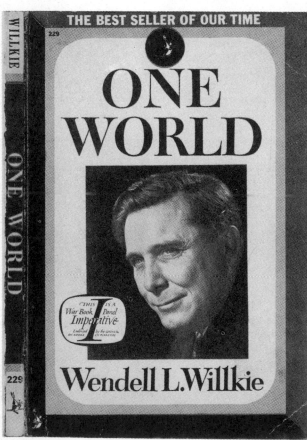

WILLKIE

229

THE BEST SELLER OF OUR TIME

ONE WORLD

THIS IS A
War Book Panel
Imperative
Endorsed by the Council
ON BOOKS IN WARTIME

Wendell L.Willkie

ONE WORLD

229

Although Roosevelt carried the election, he received 509,658 fewer votes than his 1936 mark; his plurality of 4,914,713 was the smallest for any candidate since 1916. Willkie's 22,327,226 votes were the largest number recorded for a Republican candidate. Both contestants seemed in essential agreement on goals but differed sharply on methods. Said Willkie in one of his leading campaign speeches: "There is no issue between the third-term candidate and myself on the questions of old-age pensions, unemployment insurance, collective bargaining . . . the elimination of child labor and the retention of federal relief."

Emerging from defeat with a deeply rooted sense of service to his fellow man, Willkie went on to become an international figure. Upon returning from a world tour in 1942, he paved the way for the United Nations through his book "One World", a phenomenal best seller.

Ebullient, high-powered Thomas Edmund Dewey, standard bearer of 1944 and 1948, came by his Republicanism biologically as well as philosophically. Asked by a New York Times writer "Why are you a Republican?", Dewey replied, "I believe that the Republican Party is the best instrument for bringing sound government into the hands of competent men and by this means preserving our liberty . . . But there is another reason why I am a Republican. I was born one."

Dewey was born in the apartment over this store in Owosso, Michigan, on March 24, 1902.

All the Deweys have been Republicans ever since the party was founded. Grandfather George Martin Dewey was a delegate to the historic "under the oaks" convention which drew up the first G.O.P. ticket in 1854, and his son, George Martin Dewey, Jr., won enough party backing to become an assistant to Michigan's Auditor General and, later, Postmaster of Owosso. It was almost immediately after his graduation from Columbia University's law school that Tom Dewey practically leaped into politics and went clambering up the ladder of inevitable success. By 1931 he had attracted attention not only as chairman of the New York Young Republican Club but also as an aggressive, hard-hitting lawyer. Presently U.S. District Attorney George Z. Medalie chose him as his chief assistant and placed him in charge of gang busting cases. He made good so quickly that he succeeded Medalie when the latter resigned in 1933. Two years later Democratic Governor Herbert Lehman gave Dewey his big opportunity by appointing him a special prosecutor of rackets. Only 33 years old at the time, he went into action with all the fervor of a crusader. Relentlessly and spectacularly he proceeded to indict some of the nation's most dangerous public enemies—and to capture the American imagination as no one had done since Lindbergh zoomed across the Atlantic. Of 73 cases prosecuted under his direction 72 resulted in convictions. New York County voters were so impressed they promptly elected him District Attorney, only to find him being groomed for the governorship. Less than a year afterwards the Democratic Party was panic stricken when he came within 64,000 votes of displacing Lehman. In 1942 the forty-year-old racket buster was handily elected New York's first Republican Governor in twenty years and it surprised none of his admirers to see him chosen the party's national standard bearer two years later. Although handicapped by the "don't-change-the-commander-in-chief-during-a-war" inhibition, he polled 46.2 per cent of the vote which gave F.D.R. a fourth term in the White House. In 1946 the blue-serged politico was reelected Governor of New York by the largest majority ever known to the history of the state. And in 1948 he was again made the party's Presidential nominee despite traditional reluctance to give a second chance to a defeated candidate. But what was complacently expected to be a "walkover" for Dewey turned out to be a landslide for Harry S. Truman. It was not, however, without significance that Dewey received 189 electoral votes, the greatest number scored by a Republican nominee in 16 years.

This is the Dewey family with friends and neighbors in Owosso, Michigan. Young Tom is seated in the center with hands in his lap. Directly behind him is his father, George Martin Dewey.

Dewey signing up as chief assistant to U.S. Attorney George Z. Medalie in New York City in 1931.

Reading the papers shortly after he had scored his biggest triumph as District Attorney for New York — the conviction of Tammany leader James J. Hines on charges of shielding policy game operators.

Taking the oath for his first term as Governor of New York in 1942; at right is Mrs. Dewey.

Dewey with his wife, sons, and parents.

The above demonstration took place when Dewey's name was submitted to the 1944 convention in Chicago. He was chosen the party's standard bearer on the first ballot. Governor John W. Bricker of Ohio (facing Dewey in bottom picture) was named as the Vice Presidential nominee.

Visiting the tomb of Lincoln in Illinois. Left to right above are John Knapp; Mrs. Dwight Green, wife of the Governor of Illinois; Governor Green; Governor Dewey; and Mrs. Dewey.

"That '44 Story Building"—Los Angeles Times.

"Victory Parade", in the Kansas City Star.

Although Dewey campaigned tirelessly, the nation decided it was not time to make a change. In a concluding speech, he charged Roosevelt with prolonging World War II.

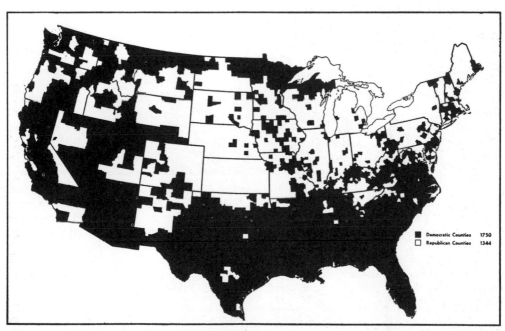

Democratic Counties 1750
Republican Counties 1344

Dewey's popular vote of 22,014,000 was 46 percent of the vote which reelected F.D.R.

"More Decontrol" by Edmund Gale in the Los Angeles Examiner was occasioned by the smashing victory of the G.O.P. in the 1946 Congressional elections. The party won majority control over the Senate and the House of Representatives for the first time since 1931. In reversing New Deal trends, the Eightieth Congress cut President Truman's requests for appropriations by $6 billion, repealed or terminated 150 wartime controls, passed the Taft-Hartley Labor-Management Relations Act, and approved the Constitutional amendment limiting future Presidents to two terms of office. In campaigning for reelection in 1948 President Harry S. Truman referred to this Congress as "that old reprobate" and "the worst in history".

Acknowledging the thunderous applause of delegates to the Philadelphia convention of June, 1948, after receiving the party's Presidential nomination for a second time. Two years earlier Dewey was reelected Governor of New York by the largest majority in the history of that state.

Below is an extract from a campaign pamphlet published by the Republican National Committee.

actions SPEAK LOUDER THAN PROMISES!

DEWEY AND WARREN
created stronger unified labor departments

To speed the efficient handling of all matters affecting citizens as wage and salary earners, Governor Dewey integrated all New York agencies dealing with such activities in the Labor Department. At the same time he increased Labor Department appropriations more than 100%.

In California, Governor Warren completely reorganized and streamlined the Department of Industrial Relations. Appropriations for the Department were substantially increased. As a result, the services and protections afforded California workers by its labor laws have been given full force and effect.

In both states, representatives of organized labor and management have been appointed to important positions, serving on Boards, Commissions and Councils which help set policies essential to sound administration and efficient operation.

By promoting teamwork between labor and management, Governors Dewey and Warren have encouraged good will and industrial harmony.

DEWEY AND WARREN
provided higher unemployment benefits

The Unemployment Compensation laws of New York and California are the best in the nation. Under Governors Dewey and Warren, benefits have been increased, waiting periods reduced, and the systems broadened to cover thousands of additional workers.

DEWEY and WARREN
have developed
better Workmen's Compensation Laws

Governors Dewey and Warren secured the enactment of legislation raising weekly benefit rates for disabling industrial injuries and occupational diseases under their States' workmen's compensation laws. Administration of the compensation laws has been  streamlined for speedy handling of claims and prompt payment of benefits to disabled workers. In addition, coverage has been extended to many workers previously unprotected.

DEWEY AND WARREN
established higher minimum wages

Under Governors Dewey and Warren, the entire minimum wage structure has been revised upward, and the enforcement provisions of their states' minimum wage laws strengthened. The number of workers covered has been greatly increased.

Thousands of additional workers have received minimum wage protection under Governors Dewey and Warren.

DEWEY AND WARREN   GET THINGS DONE for LABOR

Governor Dewey pointing out some of the sights on his dairy farm to Governor Earl Warren of California, his running mate in 1948.

"Time to Put in the First Team" (above) was circulated by the National Republican Committee.

The Dewey and Warren families in step at Pawling, New York, in the summer of 1948.

Another cartoon distributed during the 1948 campaign. It was drawn by Jay Thomas.

Elder statesmen of the 1940s: Representative Joseph Martin and Senator Arthur Vandenberg.

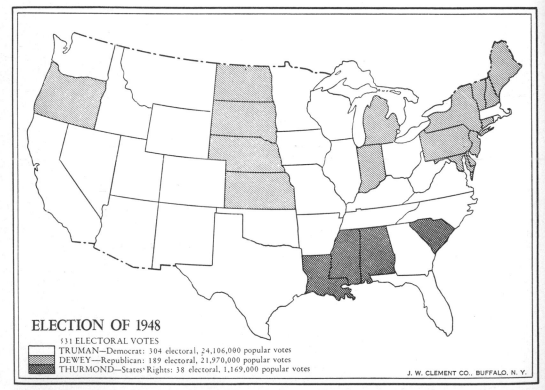

ELECTION OF 1948

531 ELECTORAL VOTES

	TRUMAN—Democrat: 304 electoral, 24,106,000 popular votes
	DEWEY—Republican: 189 electoral, 21,970,000 popular votes
	THURMOND—States' Rights: 38 electoral, 1,169,000 popular votes

J. W. CLEMENT CO., BUFFALO, N. Y.

President Harry S. Truman was reelected in an unexpected upset. However, Dewey received 189 electoral votes, the greatest number scored by a Republican candidate since 1928. Both houses of Congress were lost to the Democrats—the Senate by 54 to 42, the House by 263 to 171.

The first Republican candidate to be elected President of the United States since 1932, Dwight David Eisenhower answered a rousing call to political duty when he accepted the party's nomination in 1952. The movement to draft him for the nation's highest office was initiated some ten years earlier by an American Legion post. When the subject came up again in June 1945 he told reporters, "There's no use my denying that I'll fly to the moon, because no one has suggested it . . . The same goes for politics. I'm a soldier and I'm positive no one thinks of me as a politician." Although he let it be known that his roots were Republican, he continued to refuse to enter the political arena until convinced he could not ignore public demand.

Eisenhower's birthplace in Denison, Texas, was only a stone's throw from the town's railroad tracks.

The first photograph of Eisenhower as a baby shows him in the first row at the right. Seen in the back row are brothers Arthur (holding Earl) and Edgar.

Eisenhower with his parents and brothers in 1902. **Standing** between father and mother in the front row is Milton. In the **back** row, left to right, are Dwight, Edgar, Earl, Arthur, and Roy.

Self-denial, a virtue constantly stressed by Eisenhower's forebears, was something taken completely for granted in his family. It had to be that way because the Eisenhowers were far from well off when Dwight was a youngster. A year before he was born his dad's general store had failed and the rapidly growing family had to make the best of a very difficult situation. Not until his father obtained steady employment in an Abilene, Kansas, creamery was the family able to settle down like other folks. The Eisenhower home in Abilene, where Dwight spent most of his youth, was on the wrong side of the railroad tracks, but, as the future President recalled recently, he and his brothers didn't know this made any difference. After graduating from high school he worked at odd jobs before winning an appointment to West Point. Fresh out of the military academy, he spotted pretty Mamie Doud, and married her the day he became First Lieutenant in 1916. Further advancement was unbearably slow. He served four years before becoming a Major. And then he waited 16 years for his next promotion. Although he worked hard and was exceedingly impatient to lead troops, his life was chiefly marked by dreary tours of duty at various Army posts until 1941. Throughout his initial 27 years of service he never had a single combat command. He had barely begun to attract notice in 1935 when he was assigned to the Philippines and comparative oblivion until 1940. The first big "break" came in 1941. During maneuvers of the Third Army he established a reputation as a highly resourceful officer and his career suddenly gathered remarkable momentum. Shortly after Pearl Harbor General George C. Marshall, then the Army's Chief of Staff, summoned him to Washington, made him a temporary Brigadier General, and placed him in charge of the War Plans Division. In the summer of 1942 he was pulled up over the heads of scores of other officers and appointed a full general. By the close of 1943 he was serving as Supreme Commander of the Allied Expeditionary Forces; six months later he gave the word which launched the greatest amphibious invasion in history. Hailed as a conquering hero after Germany's defeat, he returned to the U.S., served briefly as the Army's Chief of Staff, and "retired" to the Presidency of Columbia University. However, he was no sooner ensconced at Morningside Heights than he was summoned back to Washington to preside over the Joint Chiefs of Staff, but that too turned out to be a temporary job. In 1951 he returned to Europe, this time as commander of the military organization of the North Atlantic Treaty powers. When Dwight Eisenhower entered the Presidential contest of 1952 he was a novice in politics but a professional in the art of leading men.

"Ike" (standing in the center) was in his senior year at high school when this photograph was taken with his parents and brothers Milton and Earl.

Reunion in Abilene: Roy, Arthur, Earl, Edgar, Mr. Eisenhower, Dwight, Milton, and Mrs. Eisenhower.

Newlyweds Dwight and Mamie Eisenhower in 1916. "Ike" was promoted to First Lieutenant on the same day he married Mamie Doud.

Standing in the foreground at the left, wearing a white civilian suit and straw hat, Col. Eisenhower was on hand to welcome General Douglas MacArthur to Manila in October 1935. "Ike" became an aide to MacArthur until 1940.

Accompanying Lieut. General Walter Krueger and Lieut. Col. Oliver H. Stout during Third Army maneuvers near Lake Charles, Louisiana, in August 1941.

Left: Viewing Italy's terrain with Great Britain's strategist, General Bernard L. Montgomery, in August of 1943.

Below: Visiting with British Commonwealth Prime Ministers in May 1944.

Left: Reviewing para-
troopers on the eve of
the invasion of Europe
by the Allies in 1944.

Center photo: Meeting
with top echelon offi-
cers of the Supreme
Command, Allied Expe-
ditionary Forces, in Feb-
ruary of 1945.

Below: Addressing a joint session
of Congress at the end of World
War II. Eisenhower urged the
application of "determination
. . . optimistic resolution . . .
mutual consideration" to peace-
time problems. In referring to
the sorrows of bereaved parents
and wives, he observed: "The
blackness of their grief can be
relieved only by the faith that
all this shall not happen again."

As President of Columbia University after the war, Eisenhower won respect for his liberal views.

Back again in Europe in 1951, this time as Commander-in-Chief of SHAPE, General Eisenhower watches Major General Williston Palmer (above at left) prepare to signal a mock assault during Army maneuvers near Frankfort, Germany.

Italian Prime Minister Alcide de Gasperi got some frank reactions during his visit with General Eisenhower when the latter assumed the added responsibilities of Supreme Commander for the North Atlantic Treaty Organization late in 1951.

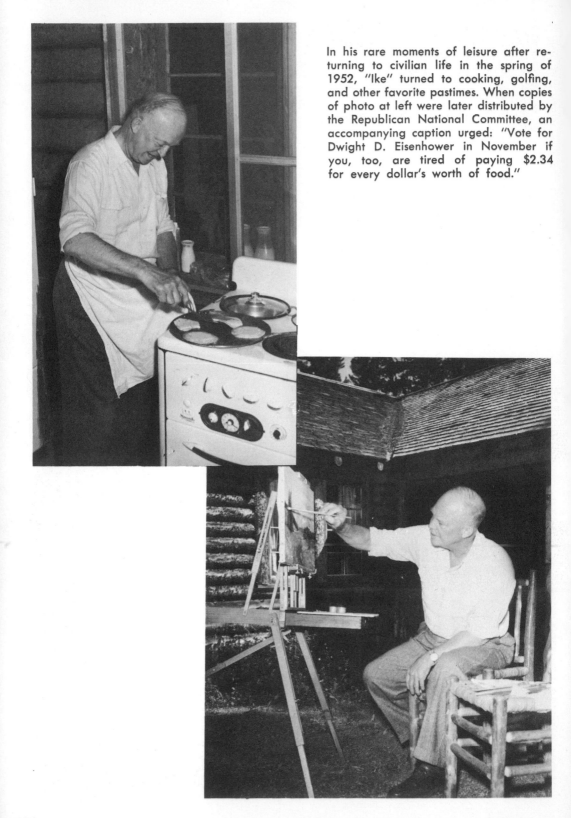

In his rare moments of leisure after returning to civilian life in the spring of 1952, "Ike" turned to cooking, golfing, and other favorite pastimes. When copies of photo at left were later distributed by the Republican National Committee, an accompanying caption urged: "Vote for Dwight D. Eisenhower in November if you, too, are tired of paying $2.34 for every dollar's worth of food."

"Ike" and Mamie with their daughter-in-law, Mrs. John Eisenhower, and grandchildren Dwight David, Susan Elaine, and Barbara Anne.

REPUBLICAN NATIONAL CONVENTION

Accepting the nomination for President at the Republican National Convention in July 1952.
A frenzy of placards hoisted high by pro-Eisenhower delegates during a demonstration.

Nominated for the Vice Presidency by acclamation, 39-year-old Senator Richard M. Nixon of California responded to convention cheers with his attractive wife.

The winners and their wives exchanging confidences at the end of the convention.

Although keenly disappointed by his failure to secure the Presidential nomination, Senator Robert A. Taft offered Eisenhower his allegiance.

"The Issues of 1952" as interpreted by Gib Crockett.

they're for you!

LET'S CLEAN HOUSE

with **IKE** and **DICK**

A **vote** for Ike and Dick is a vote **against corruption**

THEY'RE HONEST

A **vote** for Ike and Dick is a vote **for your own peace of mind**

A **vote** for Ike and Dick is a vote **against Communism**

A **vote** for Ike and Dick is a vote **for morality**

A **vote** for Ike and Dick is a vote **against high taxes and inflation**

THEY'RE SCRAPPERS

A **vote** for Ike and Dick is a vote **for prosperity without war**

THEY HAVE THE KNOW-HOW FOR GOOD GOVERNMENT

THEY'RE FAMILY MEN

These were some of the slogans highlighted in Republican National Committee literature.

Conferring with Arthur Summerfield (left), Chairman of the Republican National Committee.

Their exuberance was contagious.   Wherever they spoke, the Republican ticket grew stronger.

Waving to a crowd of well-wishers at LaPorte, Indiana, with Chief Lone Eagle.

In war-torn Korea, Marine Leonard Warner campaigned when he wasn't fighting.

Poised, bright-eyed Mrs. Eisenhower retained her natural spontaneity throughout the campaign.

Democrat Adlai Stevenson was defeated by a plurality of 6.6 million votes. "Ike" cracked the solid south, drew 6.7 million more votes than had ever been cast for any Presidential candidate.

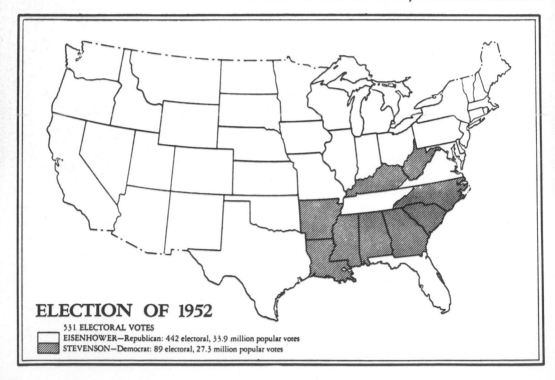

ELECTION OF 1952

531 ELECTORAL VOTES

EISENHOWER—Republican: 442 electoral, 33.9 million popular votes
STEVENSON—Democrat: 89 electoral, 27.3 million popular votes

On the threshold of his immense responsibilities as President, Eisenhower delivered an historic inaugural address. "At such a time in history," he declared, "we who are free must proclaim anew our faith. This faith is the abiding creed of our fathers. It is our faith in the deathless dignity of man, governed by eternal moral and natural laws." Concerning the challenge of Soviet communism, he spoke plainly: "We wish our friends the world over to know this above all: We face the threat — not with dread and confusion — but with confidence and conviction." Domestic problems, he emphasized, were increasingly "dwarfed by and often even created by" the problems confronting all humankind. In outlining the principles of American conduct in international affairs, he promised to "promote the conditions of peace" through strength and readiness "to engage with any and all others in joint effort to remove the causes of mutual fear", to honor "the identity and the special heritage" of all peoples, to help other free nations and to expect their help "within the limits of their resources", and to make the United Nations more effective.

"Things Begin to Happen When You Start Moving Mountains", a cartoon by Edmund Duffy, accompanied a sympathetic editorial in the Saturday Evening Post of April 4, 1953.

"Accomplishments and Tribulations" of Eisenhower's administration as visualized by James B. Ivey several months later.

"They're Using Three Platoons"—a Jim Berryman cartoon in the Washington Evening Star.

"Any time you guys are ready for the second half!" — Herblock in the Washington Post.

John Foster Dulles,
Secretary of State

George Humphrey,
Secretary of Treasury

Mrs. Oveta Culp Hobby,
Secretary of Health,
Education, and Welfare

Ezra Taft Benson,
Secretary of Agriculture

Charles E. Wilson,
Secretary of Defense

Arthur E. Summerfield,
Postmaster General

Sinclair Weeks
Secretary of Commerce

James P. Mitchell,
Secretary of Labor

Douglas McKay,
Secretary of the Interior

Herbert Brownell, Jr.,
Attorney General

Leonard W. Hall, present chairman of the Republican National Committee, was a judge and Congressman from New York.

"The New G.O.P. Chairman Reports For Duty" by Gib Crockett.

Vice President and Mrs. Richard M. Nixon in Pakistan during their trip to the Far East in August 1953.   At President Eisenhower's request, Nixon conferred with Generalissimo Chiang Kai-shek, Syngman Rhee, and the Emperor of Japan; he also surveyed the influence of Russia in the Pacific.

President Eisenhower offering the United Nations his plan for world peace and atomic control.

"There's Something About a Side Show"
— Bimrose in the Portland Oregonian.

Le affaire McCarthy as viewed by three different newspapers.

"Conscience No. 1 and No. 2".

"The Party's Problem Child".

"Close man with a razor, isn't he?" — Herblock cartoon in the Washington Post.

"But don't forget, Papa still wears the pants!"—Talburt in the Washington News.

Two interpretations of the hairline-close elections of November 2, 1954.

CREDITS

Illustrations not credited in the captions are listed below, except in the case of fugitive items. If name of artist or photographer is unknown, credit is given to original place of publication or source from which reproduction was obtained.

The following abbreviations are used—

Acme: Acme Newspictures.
Andrews: History of the Last Quarter Century in the U.S.: 1870-1895, by E. Benjamin Andrews, Scribner's, 1895.
AP: Associated Press.
APS: American Pictorial Service.
Berryman: Clifford Berryman.
Brady: Mathew Brady.
CI: Currier and Ives.
French: Herbert E. French.
Gardner: Alexander Gardner.
Gros: T.R. in Cartoon, by Raymond Gros, Saalfield Publishing Co., 1910.
HE: Harris and Ewing.
HW: Harper's Weekly.
INP: International News Photos.
Keppler: Joseph Keppler.
LC: Library of Congress.
Leslie's: Frank Leslie's Illustrated Newspaper.
Nast: Thomas Nast.
Paine: Thomas Nast, His Period and His Pictures, by Albert Bigelow Paine, Macmillan, 1904.
RNC: Republican National Committee.
Rogers: William Allen Rogers.
Robinson: They Voted for Roosevelt, by Edgar E. Robinson, Stanford Press, 1947
Shaw: Abraham Lincoln, His Path to the Presidency, by Albert Shaw, Review of Reviews Corporation, 1930.
UU: Underwood and Underwood.

WES: Washington Evening Star.
WW: Wide World.

Credits are listed in terms of appearance left to right and top to bottom, unless otherwise indicated.

9   Wisconsin Historical Society; Shaw, vol. 1, p. 170.
10 Wisconsin Historical Society
11 Jackson Public Library
12 N.Y. Historical Society
13 F. O. C. Darley; History of Kansas, John N. Holloway
14 Leslie's, Dec. 15, 1855; Leslie's, July 26, 1856
15 Leslie's, Feb. 16, 1856
16 J. L. Magee
17 LC
18- APS
19
20 George Caleb Bingham
21 Charles Rockwood
22 Brady?
23 Meserve Collection; T. Buchanan Read
24 J. McNevin; LC
25 Fremont's Memoirs, 1887; Fremont: Pathmarker of the West, Allan Nevins, 1939, p. 211
26 Leslie's, July 5, 1856; Huntington Library
27 LC
28 Louis Maurer (bottom)
29 LC
30 J. C. Buttre (top)
31 - 32 Gardner
33 APS
34 LC; Brady
35 - 37 APS
38 Frank Bellew; Joseph Beale
39 HW, 1860; APS
40 HW, May 19, 1860; RNC
41 W. H. Rease; Illinois State Historical Library
42 - 43 HW, Oct. 13, 1860
44 - 45 CI
46 Shaw, vol. 2, pp. 85 and 101

47   CI; LC
48   Shaw, vol. 2, p. 61; vol. 1, p. 211
49   CI (bottom)
50   HW, March 9, 1861 (top); APS
51   Leslie's, March 16, 1861; HW, 1861
52   Nast in Shaw, vol. 2, p. 267; LC
53   APS; LC
54   LC (bottom)
55   Shaw, vol. 2, p. 270; Yankee Notions, 1861
56   HW, Nov. 26, 1864; Vanity Fair, March 9, 1861
57   Adelbert John Volck
58   B. B. Russell
59   Department of Agriculture
60   Nebraska State Historical Society
61   Department of Interior
62   Federal Reserve Bank of Boston (top)
63   Gardner; National Archives
64   LC; A. R. Ward in HW, 1862
65 - 66   Department of Interior
67 - 68   LC
69   Alexander H. Ritchie; APS
70   National Archives
71   APS
72   LC; M. W. Siebert
73   J. L. Magee
74   LC; HW, Sept. 3, 1864
75   APS; CI
76   Gardner
77   National Archives; LC
78   CI; Nast in Paine, p. 103
79   HW, April 15, 1865; Pur May 6, 1865
80   S. M. Fassett; APS
81   Brady
82   J. C. Buttre; Gardner?
83   National Park Service
84   National Park Service; Leslie's, Jan. 6, 1865
85   Brady
86 - 87   LC
88   HW, Oct. 14, 1865; I. A. Wetherby
89   HW, Nov. 3, 1866
90   APS

91   HW, Aug. 4, 1866
92   APS; HW, Sept. 1, 1866
93   A. H. Ritchie
94   Emanuel Leutze; Richard E. Harrison
95   Theodore R. Davis in HW, April 11, 1868; CI
96   APS; Robert Dudley, Metropolitan Museum of Art
97   Union Pacific Railroad
98   LC
99   APS
100   Frederick Remington; APS
101   APS
102   Department of Interior
103   A. R. Waud in HW, 1869
104   W. L. Sheppard in HW, 1868; HW, July 10, 1869; CI
105   A. Bogardus
106   Leslie's, 1865; LC
107   Gardner
108   Ulysses S. Grant III Collection
109   LC
110   Mezzotint by John Sartain after painting by William Cogswell
111   Leslie's, June 13, 1869; Kellogg and Bulkley
112   CI lithograph by J. Cameron; Nast in HW, Oct. 31, 1868
113   APS; CI lithograph by Thomas Worth (bottom)
114   APS (top)
114 - 115   Nast in HW, Oct., 1868
115   Nast in HW, Sept. 1868 (top)
116   National Archives
117   HW, 1869; LC
118   CI; James E. Taylor in Leslie's, 1869
119   APS; LC
120   Howard in HW, Sept. 16, 1871
121   Nast in Paine, p. 212; Nast in HW, Oct. 5, 1872
122   Nast in HW; LC
123   APS; Census Bureau
124   CI
125   APS
126   Nast in Paine
127   LC
128   Nast in HW, Nov. 23, 1872

129 HW, March 22, 1873; James E. Taylor in Leslie's, 1873

130 APS; Nast in Paine, p. 211

131 Reddington and Shaffer Studio

133 Nast in Paine, p. 315

134 Leslie's, 1876; Nast in Paine, p. 327

135 Frank Bellew in HW; HW, Nov. 7, 1874

136 Brady; National Park Service

137 National Park Service

138 American Oleograph Co.

140 APS; HW, May 27, 1876

141 APS; LC; HW, May 27, 1876

142 John C. McRae

143 - 144 Hayes Memorial Library

145 HW, 1876; Hayes Memorial Library

146 Brady; Hayes Memorial Library

147 CI

148 Nast in HW, July 8, 1876

150 Leslie's, 1876; Illustrated London Daily News, Dec. 19, 1876

151 Nast in HW, Oct. 28, 1876; Nast in HW, March 24, 1877; Hayes Memorial Library

152 LC; Bureau of Engraving and Printing; Hagstrom Co.

153 Leslie's, Dec. 2, 1876; Nast in HW, Feb. 17, 1877

154 LC; Leslie's, March 24, 1877

155 Brady

156 L. E. Walker in HW, 1877; Leslie's, 1877

157 Brady

158 HW, Oct. 13, 1877; Puck, May 12, 1880

159 C. S. Reinhart in HW, Oct. 20, 1877; HW, March 17, 1877

160 Nast in Paine, p. 363; HW, 1880

161 W. M. Rouzee in HW, Jan. 22, 1881

162 Keppler in Puck, 1877; C. S. Reinhart in HW, Oct. 20, 1877

163 Nast in HW, April, 1878; APS

164 APS; Leslie's, Jan. 8, 1881

165 Leslie's, 1878; I. P. Pranishnikoff in HW

166 Keppler in Puck, Oct. 13, 1880; APS

167 Gray Parker in Daily Graphic, 1877

168 Samuel M. Stevens

169 RNC

170 Arony Studio

171 APS; Leslie's, 1881

172 LC; Kurz and Allison

173 - 174 LC

175 C. D. Mosher; Nast in HW, Sept. 27, 1879

177 CI; Keppler in Puck, Sept. 29, 1880

178 CI

179 Nast in HW, Nov. 1880

180 - 182 Leslie's, 1881

183 Nast in HW, 1881

184 Keppler in Puck, April 28, 1880; Nast in HW, May 14, 1881

185 LC

186 APS; LC; Nast in Paine, p. 447; Nast in Paine, p. 448

187 Leslie's, July 16, 1881

188 W. Shinkle in HW, 1881; APS

189 RNC

190 Daniel Huntington, Frick Art Reference Library

191 Vermont Historical Society; LC

192 Leslie's, 1881

193 HW, 1884

194 Nast in Paine, p. 44; Keppler in Puck, Oct. 5, 1881

195 - 196 LC

197 LC; Henry Linton

198 Leslie's, Sept. 16, 1882

199 Department of Labor

200 - S. D. Butcher, Nebraska State
201 Historical Society

202 Corcoran Art Gallery; N.Y. Historical Society

203 - 204 APS

205 Mora Studio

206 James Archer, National Gallery of Art

207 APS; S. S. Cox in Andrews, vol. 2, p. 67

208 APS (1880 item); HW, June 14, 1884
209 Leslie's, June 14, 1884; Brady?
210 H. M. Kelley
211 Keppler in Puck, 1880
212 Macbriar; Town Topics, Sept. 20, 1884
213 LC
214 W. H. Dodd Co.; Frank Beard in Judge, Sept. 27, 1884
215 J. A. Wales in Puck; Grant Hamilton in Judge, July 12, 1884
216 Keppler in Puck, June 18, 1884
217 Andrews, vol. 2, p. 86 (bottom)
218 Pan American Union
219 Brady
220 Eastman Johnson, National Gallery of Art
221 Kurz and Allison; Shober Lithograph Co.
223 Chas. Parker; George Prince
224 French; Pach Studio; CI
225 Leslie's, Nov. 10, 1888; APS
226 Kurz and Allison; Frank Adams in Leslie's, June 30, 1888
227 Charles M. Bell (top)
228 R. K. Bonine; Brown Bros.
229 George Millner Collection
230 French; Bernard Gillam in Judge, Sept. 8, 1888
231 Bureau of Engraving and Printing; APS
232 Gillert Studio; Clement Co.
233 George Prince; LC; Berryman in WES, July 1939
234 Kansas Historical Society
235 Nebraska State Historical Sociey; J. C. H. Grabill
236 Leslie's, Aug. 11, 1892; HW, June 11, 1892; Arony Studio
237 Oklahoma Historical Society
238 - 239 Bureau of Land Management, Department of Interior
240 Charles Gram in HW, 1886
242 N.Y. Edison Co.
243 RNC
244 Frances B. Johnston

245 Frances B. Johnston; LC; Universal Photo Art Co.
246 APS; Ehrgott, Ferbriger and Co.
247 Edwards, Deutsch, and Wettman Co.
248 Leslie's, July 11 and June 25, 1896
249 Gillespie, Metzer, and Kelley
250 APS; Puck, 1886
251 J. S. Pughe in Puck; HW, Aug. 29, 1896
252 Norman Photo Co. (Hanna); Meyer Studio
253 Robert Bracklow
254 LC
255 - 256 George Prince
257 Strohmeyer and Wyman
258 Charles M. Bell; Robert Bracklow
259 Rogers in HW; National Archives
261 Rufus F. Zogbaum
262 de Thulstrup in HW; APS
263 APS
264 Theobald Chartran, Frick Art Reference Library (top)
265 Sacramento Daily Bee, May 25, 1898; William Rau
266 APS; HW, Aug. 18, 1898
267 J. E. Puroy; APS
268 Dalrymple in Puck, April 18, 1900; APS
269 George Prince; APS
270 Rogers in HW, 1900; APS
271 F. Victor Gillam in Judge, Nov. 10, 1900
272 F. Cresson Schell in Leslie's, Nov. 24, 1900 (bottom)
273 Bell's National Photo Gallery; Frances B. Johnston
274 J. H. Harper; HW, July 27, 1889
276 LC; Bureau of Public Roads
277 LC; Bureau of Public Roads
278 - 280 Bureau of Land Management
281 Theodore Roosevelt Memorial Association
282 T. Dart Walker in Leslie's, Sept. 21, 1900
283 RNC

284 Rockwood Photo Co.
285 W. C. Morris in Gros, p. 350 (top and bottom); American Museum of Natural History (center)
286 APS; George G. Bain; Puck, Nov. 10, 1886; Nast in HW, April 19, 1884
287 UU
288 LC
289 Theobald Chartran, National Gallery of Art; Pach Bros.
290 William Dinwiddie
291 W. G. Read
292 Berryman in Washington Post, 1902
293 Kermit Roosevelt; LC
294 John T. McCutcheon in Theodore Roosevelt in Cartoons, 1910
296 N.Y. Evening Mail, July 27, 1904
297 S. L. Stein
298 - 299 RNC
300 Pach Bros.; Kurz and Allison
301 UU
302 Rogers in HW, March 4, 1905; George Prince
303 Rogers in HW; L. D. Bradley in Chicago Daily News; Gregg in Atlanta Constitution; N.Y. Globe
304 Department of Labor
305 Department of Agriculture
306 HE; National Park Service
307 National Park Service (top)
308 Bureau of Land Management
310 Allemano in U.S.A.: An American History, by Harold U. Faulkner, Harper, 1945, p. 376 (bottom)
311 Alfred Stieglitz, Philadelphia Museum of Art
312 American Musuem of Natural History; Smithsonian Institution
313 Air Force; Smithsonian Institution; Air Force
315 Gros, p. 224; U.S. Naval Academy
316 APS
317 UU; APS

318 UU; LC
319 P. B. McCord in Newark Evening News; Pan American Union
320 LC; Pueblo Star Journal
321 Pach Bros.
322 Detroit Photographic Co.
323 RNC
324 - 325 LC
326 Waldo Fawcett; Clinedinst
327 Clinedinst; Elizabeth Kern Collection
328 Keppler in Puck, April 24, 1908; W. P. Canfield; L. D. Bradley
330 Whiting View Co.)top)
331 Kurz and Allison; APS
332 UU (top)
333 UU; Punch, Nov. 11, 1908
334 Pictorial News Co.; Keystone View Co.
335 UU; Pictorial News Co.
336 UU; Netman Studio; Rogers in N.Y. Herald, March 12, 1909
337 HE; George T. Woodward
338 Department of Interior; INP
339 John T. McCutcheon in Chica Tribune, Jan. 18, 1912; McCutcheon in Chicago Tribune, May 28, 1912
340 Smithsonian Institution
341 Bureau of Public Roads
342 Boardman Robinson in N.Y. Tribune, Feb. 27, 1912; Art Young in Puck, 1912
343 J. M. Glackens in Puck, May, 1912; Marcus in N.Y. Times, June 23, 1912
344 Punch, 1912
345 Columbia University
346 HW, Nov. 16, 1912 (top)
347 HE
348 Gustave Lorey
349 Mrs. Chauncey Waddell Collection
350 Bachrach
351 Waddell Collection
352 C. Curtis (bottom)
353 UU; Waddell Collection
354 Seldman Photo Service
355 Waddell Collection

356	Waddell Collection; Rollin Kirby in N.Y. World
357	Frederick J. Weber; UU; Waddell Collection
358	WES, July 29, 1916; UU
359	Albany Knickerbocker Press; Clement Co.
360	HE (bottom)
361	RNC
362 - 363	French
364	C. E. Coomer; APS; Edmonston; French
365 - 367	French
368	French; F. T. Richards in Life, Aug. 5, 1920; French
369	French (bottom)
370	French
371	APS (top)
372	French;APS
373-	French
373 - 377	French
379	French
380	French; National Archives
381	National Archives; Larry Keys in Columbus Citizen, Feb. 7, 1922; Harry Westerman in Ohio State Journal, June 11, 1923
382 - 385	French
386	French (bottom)
387	RNC
388	French; Hirst Milhollen
389	Bain; French; P & A Photo
390	INP; APS
391 - 394	French
395	Howard Chandler Christy; French; Boston Post
396 - 397	French
398	John T. McCutcheon in Chicago Tribune; Rollin Kirby in N.Y. World
399	French; Post Office Department
400	Berryman in WES, March 1924; Rogers in Washington Post, April 19, 1924
401	APS (top)
402 - 403	French
404	Berryman in WES, 1925 (top)
405	Berryman in WES, 1925; Rollin Kirby in N.Y. World
406	Department of Labor

407	French
408	French; National Archives; French
409	APS (bottom)
410	APS (top)
411	RNC
412	French
413	APS; Collier's, Feb. 20, 1932; French
414	APS; UU; French
415	French
416	N.Y. Herald Tribune, April 27, 1927 (bottom)
417	Berryman in WES, 1928
418	French (top)
420	RNC
421	N.Y. Herald Tribune, Nov. 7, 1928
423	Signal Corps, U.S. Army
424 - 426	French
427	United Air Lines
428	French; Berryman in WES, Oct. 10, 1931
429	J. N. Ding in N.Y. Herald Tribune, May 12, 1929
430	French (top)
432	French; Department of Labor
433	N.Y. Times, Dec. 2, 1930; Brooklyn Times, Oct. 20, 1930; Rochester Times-Union, Oct. 9, 1930
434	RNC (top)
435	RNC
436	Fifty-nine Cents of Your Dollar, T. R. Carskadon, Public Affairs Committee; The United States, Louis Hacker and Rudolph Modley, Modern Age, 1937, p. 83
437	U.S.A., Harold U. Faulkner, Harper, 1945, p. 418; APS
438	APS
439	RNC
440	HE
441 - 446	RNC
447	Navy Department
448 - 449	RNC
451	Marcus in N.Y. Times; Hutton in Philadelphia Inquirer
452	RNC; Robinson, p. 35
453	RNC
454	Movietone News

455 - 456   Mrs. Willkie's Collection
457   WW
458 - 459   Albert T. Reid
460   AP; INP
461   AP; Seidman Photo Service
462   F. A. Russo
463   RNC; Acme
464   RNC
465   INP (top)
466   Robinson, p. 38 (top)
467   Halsman
468   HE
469   Acme
470   RNC; Acme
471   Acme
472 - 473   RNC
474   INP
475   RNC; Robinson, p. 39
476   Los Angeles Examiner, Nov. 8, 1946
477   INP (top)
478 - 479   RNC
480   HE; Clement Co.
481   George Tames, N.Y. Times

482   Fabian Bachrach
483 - 485   Eisenhower Foundation
486 - 489   Department of Army
490   Warman, Columbia University
491   Acme
492   Claude Powe
495 - 496   WW
497   WES (top)
498   WW
499   United Press
500   Clement Co. (bottom)
501   Harry Goodman in WES
502   WES, July 19, 1953 (bottom)
504   HE (Dulles)
505   HE (Summerfield);   Fabian Bachrach (Weeks)
506   WES, April 13, 1953
507   Pakistan Embassy
508   United Nations, Washington Office
509   Hesse in St. Louis Globe-Democrat; Justus in Minneapolis Star (bottom)

INDEX

Adams, Charles Francis, 426
Adams, F. P., 457
Agriculture Department, 59
agriculture, 232, 383, 419, 430, 432
Alabama Claims, 121
Alaska, 94, 277
Alger, Russell A., 258
Allison, William B., 214
Arizona, 338
Arthur, Chester, 52, 177, 189-204, 212, 214
Banks, Nathaniel, 15, 39
Bates, Edward, 39, 58
Belknap, William F., 134
Bell, John, 39, 45
Benson, Ezra T., 504
Beveridge, Albert, 328
Black Friday, 119
Blaine, James G., 166, 170, 175, 184, 185, 205-218
Blair, Frank P., 113

Blair, Montgomery, 58
Bliss, Cornelius N., 258
Bonaparte, Charles J., 302
Bone, Scott, 385
Borah, William E., 369
Borie, Adolph E., 117
Boutwell, George S., 18, 117
Bovay, Alvin E., 10
Brady, John R., 192
Brady, Mathew, see 518
Breckenridge, John C., 45-49
Briand, Aristide, 379, 380
Bricker, John W., 473
Brown, B. Gratz, 18, 127
Brown, John, 13
Brown, Walter F., 426
Brownell, Herbert, Jr., 505
Bryan, William Jennings, 250, 271, 308, 369
Buckner, S. P., 113
Bull Moose symbol, 346

Butler, Benjamin, 58, 130
Butler, Nicholas Murray, 345, 369
Butterfield, Daniel, 119
Cameron, J. Donald, 214
Cameron, Simon, 39, 58
Cannon, Joseph, 336, 383
Capper-Volstead Act, 383
Catholic vote, 217
Chase, Salmon P., 39, 58, 62, 84
Chandler, W. E., 214
Chinese labor, 176
Churchill, Winston, 488
Civil Service, 122, 148, 162, 187, 233, 437
Clay, Cassius M., 39
Cleveland, Grover, 214, 227, 236, 256, 286
Colby, Bainbridge, 446
Colfax, Schuyler, 86, 111, 113, 117

Commerce Department, 416

Conkling, Roscoe, 152, 166, 184, 186

conservation, 306, 307

Coolidge, Calvin, 367, 372-375, 386-410, 415, 417

Copperheads, 120

Cortelyou, George B., 302

Cox, Jacob D., 117

Cox, James M., 368, 372

Crane, Murray, 369

Creswell, John A., 117

Crittenden Compromise, 50

Currier and Ives, see 518

Curtis, Charles, 366, 402, 417, 424

Custer, George A., 136

Daugherty, Harry M., 375, 398

Davis, James J., 375, 396, 406, 426

Dawes, Rufus, 402-405, 432

Day, William R., 258

Dayton, William L., 27, 30

Democratic Party, 331, 463

Denby, Edwin, 375

Dennison, William, 86

Depew, Chauncey, 224

depression of 1929, 430-433

Devens, Charles, 157

Dewey, George, 261, 265

Dewey, Thomas E., 467-480

Dingley Act, 274

disarmament, 378-381

dollar, first, 62

Douglas, Lewis, 446

Douglas, Stephen A., 38, 45-49

Dulles, John F., 504

Edison, Thomas Alva, 203-204, 365

Edmunds, George F., 214

education, 61, 148

Eisenhower, Dwight D., 481-509

electric power projects, 338, 427

elephant, first appearance as G.O.P. symbol, 132

Emancipation Proclamation, 69-70

Elkins, Stephen B., 232

Ellsworth, Ephraim, 58

Ely, Joseph M., 446

Evarts, William M., 157, 166

Everett, Edward, 46

Fair, James G., 108

Fairbanks, Charles W., 328, 354, 355, 300

Fall, Albert B., 375, 398

Fenton, Reuben, 126

Federal Farm Board, 430

Federal Reserve Board, 432

Fess, Simeon, 381, 434

Fessenden, William, 86

Fish, Hamilton, 19, 117, 121

Fisher, Walter L., 337

Food and Drug Act, 305

Foraker, Joseph, 248, 252, 328, 362

Ford, Henry, 365

foreign trade, 164, 167

Foster, Charles, 232

Foster, John W., 232

Foster, Lafayette, 86

Freeman, Daniel, 60

Frelinghuysen, Frederick T., 214

Fremont, John C., 21-30, 39

Free Soilers, 9, 16

Gage, Lyman J., 258

Garfield, James A., 52, 169-188

Garfield, James R., 174, 302

geological surveys, 119, 165

Gompers, Samuel, 251

Good, James, 426

Grant, Ulysses S., 105-142, 148, 170, 175, 214, 258

Great Britain, 121

Greeley, Horace, 10, 44, 46, 125-128

Green, Dwight, 474

Green, William, 432

Gresham, Walter Q., 214

Griggs, John W., 258

Grow, Rep., 17

Hall, Leonard W., 506

Hallwagon, Edward, 335

Hamlin, Hannibal, 39, 58

Hancock, Winfield Scott, 113, 178-179

Hanna, Marcus, 245, 252, 281, 297

Harding, Warren G., 361-386, 391

Harlan, James, 86

Harrison, Benjamin, 52, 52, 214, 219-242

Hawaii, 135, 266

Hay, John, 267, 297, 320

Hayes, Rutherford B., 52, 143-168, 177

Hays, Will, 367, 369, 375

Hitchcock, Frank H., 337

Hoar, Ebenezer R., 337

Hoar, George F., 133, 214

Hobart, Garrett A., 249, 254

Hobby, Oveta C., 502, 504

Holmes, Oliver Wendell, 394

Homestead Act and benefits, 41, 60, 102, 133, 200-201, 229, 237-239, 278-280, 308 (see also western settlement)

Hoover, Herbert, 375, 386, 396, 411-438

Hughes, Charles Evans, 335, 347-360 375, 379, 381, 386, 396

Humphrey, George, 504

Hunt, William, 185

Hurley, Patrick J., 434

Huston, Claudius H., 424

Hyde, Arthur W., 426

immigration, 135, 164, 184, 202, 310, 311

Indians, 77, 136, 137, 161, 399

inflation, 130 (see also depression)

Ingalls, John J., 214
Ingersoll, Robert G., 212
interstate commerce, 339
inventions, 203 (see also electricity and telephone)
Jackson convention, 11
James, Thomas L., 185
Japan, 314, 315, 318
Johnson, Andrew, 71, 77, 78, 81-104, 113
Johnson, Hiram, 343, 348, 368, 400
Kansas, 9, 12, 14, 16, 50, 234
Kansas-Nebraska Bill, 9
Kellogg, Frank, 396, 397, 408, 426
Keppler, Joseph, see 518
Key, David M., 157
Kieran, John, 457
Kinkhead, J. H., 108
Kirkwood, Thomas J., 185
Knapp, John, 474
Knox, Frank, 446-448
Knox, Philander C., 337
Krueger, Walter, 487
Ku Klux Klan, 90-91, 120, 158, 370, 401
labor, 124, 198-199, 250-251, 304, 390, 406, 477
Labor Department, 199, 210, 339, 406
La Follette, Robert M., 230, 401
Lamont, Robert P., 426
land, see Homestead Act
Land Grant College Act, 61
Landon, Alfred M., 439-452
Lewis, John L., 406
Lincoln, Abraham, 31-80
Lincoln, Robert Todd, 185, 214, 382
Lindbergh, Charles, 407
Lodge, Henry Cabot, 366, 383
Logan, John A., 111, 209, 210, 214
Long, John D., 258
loyalty, 354
Lowden, Frank, 369

Lowell, James Russell, 160
MacArthur, Douglas, 487
Mackay, John
MacVeagh, Franklin, 337
MacVeagh, Wayne, 185
Mann-Elkins Act, 339
Martin, Joseph, 480
McCarthy, Joseph, 502, 509
McClellan, George, 72-73
McClernand, John, 63
McCrary, George, 157
McCulloch, Hugh, 86
McKay, Douglas, 505
McLean, John, 39
McNary, Charles, 462
Medalie, George Z., 469, 470
Mediation Board, 406
Mellon, Andrew W., 375, 386, 396, 397, 425, 426
Metcalf, Victor H., 302
Meyer, George Von L., 302, 337
Milburn, James G., 281
Miller, John F., 214
Mills, Roger Q., 230
Missouri Compromise, 13
Mitchell, James P., 505
Mitchell, William D., 426
money policies, 130, 133, 163, 249
Montgomery, Bernard, 488
Morrill, Justin S., 61
Morton, Levi P., 224, 226
Muir, John, 307
Myers, William Starr, 232
Nagel, Charles, 337
Nast, Thomas, see 518
Navy, 133, 197, 261, 314, 378, 380
Nebraska, 9, 235
New, Harry S., 396
Newton, Isaac, 59
Nineteenth Amendment, 371
Nixon, Richard M., 495, 498, 507
Noble, John W., 232
Nobel Prize, 319, 321

Norris-La Guardia Act, 432
Oglesby, Richard J., 19
Oklahoma, 229, 237-239, 278-280
Open Door policy, 267
Panama Canal, 267, 316-317
Pan American Union, 218, 319
Palmer, Williston, 491
Parker, Alton B., 299
patronage, 156, 162, 186 (see also Civil Service)
Pendleton, George H., 113
Pennington, William, 39
Pershing, John J., 377, 379
Philadelphia, 276
Philippine Islands, 262-263
Pinkerton, Allan, 63
Pittsburgh, 15
Platt, Thomas, 186
polygamy, 148
population growth, 310 (see also immigration)
Populists, 234
Post Office Department, 197, 339, 399
Powell, John W., 119
prices, 270
Proctor, W. C., 369
Progressive Party, 343, 401
Prohibition, 376
Quay, Matthew, 233
railroads, 65-67, 97-99, 133, 276, 438
Rankin, Jeanette, 359
Rawlins, John A., 117
Reclamation Act, 307
Reconstruction Finance Corporation, 432
Reed, James A., 446
Reed, Thomas B., 233
Reid, Whitelaw, 236
Republican, origin of term, 10
Ripon meetings, 9-10
roads, 341, 436
Robinson, George P., 214

Rogers, William A., see
  518
Roosevelt Dam, 338
Roosevelt, Franklin D.,
  372, 440, 444, 449
Roosevelt, Theodore R.,
  233, 259, 269, 283-
  322, 328-333, 342-344
Root, Elihu, 192, 302,
  319, 320, 321, 328,
  394
Rum, Romanism, and Re-
  bellion, 217
Rust, Jeremiah M., 232
Russia, 135, 318
Schauzer, Carlo, 380
Schenck, Robert, 86
Schurz, Carl, 126, 157,
  160, 215
Senate, 131, 339, 405
Seventeenth Amendment,
  339
Seward, William H., 46,
  48, 58, 89, 93, 94
Seymour, Horatio, 112,
  113, 115
Sherman, James S., 331,
  336
Sherman, John 86, 157,
  214, 231, 303
Sixteenth Amendment,
  339
Slavery, 9, 13, 16, 69-70,
  75, 183
Smith, Alfred E., 419,
  421, 446
Smith, C. B., 58
Smith, Charles E., 258
soil conservation, 307
Spanish-American War,
  259-266, 290, 291
Speed, James, 86
steam roller, 343

Stevens, Thaddeus, 86
Stimson, Henry L., 337,
  426
St. Lawrence waterway,
  416
Stone, Harlan F., 396
Stout, Oliver H., 487
Straus, Oscar S., 302
submarine, 315
suffrage, 371
Summerfield, Arthur E.,
  498, 505
Sumner, Charles, 16, 19,
  46, 174
Taft-Hartley Act, 476
Taft, Robert, 326-327,
  463, 496
Taft, William Howard,
  302, 323-346, 357,
  382, 386, 397, 426
Tammany, 133
Taney, Roger B., 52
tariff, 41, 133, 225, 230,
  244, 250, 274, 336,
  368
taxes, 120, 339
Teapot Dome, 375
Thirteenth Amendment,
  75
Thompson, Richard W.,
  157
Tilden, Samuel, 151, 159,
  212
Tipton, Andrew, 126
Tracey, Benjamin F., 232
Truman, Harry S., 497
Trumbull, Lyman, 19. 126
trusts, 231, 303, 339
unions, 108, 437 (see also
  labor)
United Nations, 508
Vandenberg, Arthur, 463,
  480

Waite, Morrison R., 155
Wallace, Henry C., 375,
  396
Wanamaker, John, 232
Warren, Earl, 478, 479
Washburn, Elihu B., 18
Washington Treaty, 121
Webb, James W., 46
Weeks, John W., 375,
  396
Weeks, Sinclair, 505
Wells, Gideon, 58
western settlement, 99-
  102, 119, 200, 232
Wheeler, William A., 147,
  152
Whigs, 9, 10
White, Horace, 38, 53,
  156, 195, 257
Wickersham, George W.,
  337
Wilbur, Curtis D., 396
Wilbur, Ray Lyman, 425,
  426
Wiley, Harvey W., 305
Willkie, Wendell L., 453-
  466
Windom, William, 185
Wilson, Charles E., 504
Wilson, Henry, 18, 86,
  124
Wilson, James L., 258,
  281, 302, 337
women, employment of,
  64, 199
women's rights, 148, 371
Wood, Leonard, 357,
  366, 369
Work, Hubert, 396, 424,
  425
Wright brothers, 313